Codes *of* Conduct

Codes
of
Conduct

Race, Ethics, and the
Color of Our Character

Karla F. C.
Holloway

#wordwork 2016
12/8

R
Rutgers University Press
New Brunswick, New Jersey

Library of Congress Cataloging-in-Publication Data

Holloway, Karla F. C.
    Codes of conduct : race, ethics, and the color of our character / Karla
F. C. Holloway.
        p.   cm.
    Includes bibliographical references and index.
    ISBN 0-8135-2155-6
    1. Afro-Americans—Race identity. 2. Ethnicity—United States.
3. United States—Race relations. 4. Race relations in literature.
5. Ethnicity in literature. 6. American literature—Afro-American
authors—History and criticism. 7. Black English in literature.
I. Title.
E185.625.H65   1995
305.896'073—dc20   94-32738
                                                            CIP

British Cataloging-in-Publication information available

For Ayana Tamu and Bem Kayin;
but especially for B K

Contents

CHAPTER THREE

The Moral Lives of Children   137

EPILOGUE

A Storied Life   191

Illustrations

Acknowledgments

I am grateful for the encouraging and challenging audiences at the University of North Carolina at Chapel Hill, North Carolina State University, Duke University, and the University of Pennsylvania who responded to the manuscript in progress with enthusiasm and support. I also acknowledge, with thanks, *Women's Studies: An Interdisciplinary Journal*, and Duke University Press, which published *Subjects and Citizens: Nations, Race, and Gender from Ooroonoko to Anita Hill*. Portions of this manuscript appear in those publications.

The supportive conversations I had with many colleagues and with my students were especially critical to the evolution of this manuscript and I am appreciative of them all, but I want to give special thanks to Houston Baker, Cathy Davidson, Trudier Harris, Helen Houston, Lauren Jones, Sheila McKoy, Joyce Pettis, and Eve Sedgwick whose friendship and loving concern are a blessing. The Friday Night Women, my sisters, have been unfailing in their loving and strengthening community.

This book would not have been written without the constancy and critical acumen of Maurice O. Wallace, my intellectual and spiritual touchstone, whose care and thoughtful generosity, and whose rigorous intellect and compassionate attention I value immeasurably. The precocious and precious wisdom of my wonderful daughter, Ayana—who reads for me with an insight that is both careful and critical, and who brings her sensitive scientific spirit to all of our conversations (those both literary and fractal-filled)—is a constant blessing. The completion of this manuscript is in great measure due to my husband Russell's gently loving and persistent nudge to persevere—a quality he makes certain is always within my reach. And finally, the friendship and deep consideration, as well as the fine and supremely practiced editorial guidance that Leslie Mitchner of Rutgers University Press has generously shared with me, has enriched my life and my spirit.

A Common Sense, A Mother Wit: Reflections on Ethics and Ethnicity

"Act your age, not your color." I turned only slightly; but just enough to make certain I had not imagined these words—that they had actually been spoken by someone and had not slipped away from a distant, childhood memory. But the force of what was essentially a quiet rebuke was too insistent for me to have imagined it. Yes. There they were. The mother's hand circled her son's small upper arm, and she was still bending over him with a posture designed to trap his small body with her own. She would succeed, I was certain. And it was not because of how she held him; it was the accompanying rebuke that made me sure his behavior would not be repeated. He would recognize that she meant for him to stop running through the lobby, collecting bank slips and free candies and swinging the thick, velvet-roped aisle markers as if they were jump ropes on a playground. I was fully attentive now, and although I held my spot in the credit union line, I shifted my gaze toward the mother and son in the next line, watching the non-event that was not happening next to me.

What she told him was to make certain that nothing happened. The purpose of her admonition was to nudge this youngster's activity into passivity, and to assure that no particular attention was drawn to them in that line of mostly white people, herself, and her child. It was not the volume of her words that gained my attention; it was their familiarity. After all, the admonition required subtlety if it was to work the way it was intended. It was not meant to be loud, just effective. It was likely that her words dissolved as they drifted past the other customers waiting in line, but they stopped fully formed when they got to my place because I could give them a text and because I held a memory of them. She snatched his arm at the beginning of what was to have been his second trip down the aisle, issued the rebuke, and held him in place.

Sufficiently chastised, the youngster in the credit union kept to his place. His mother completed her business and left the lobby quietly. I too completed my task and also left quietly—burdened by the association between color and character her words had recalled to me. Vignettes from my own childhood replaced the scene that did not happen in the line next to mine.

Those words, whispered with an intensity only a black child understands, initiate a public behavior firmly attached to a conviction that our places in line are easily jeopardized. So powerful and persuasive was its pronouncement that, as children, we even conscripted it for our own use. It was an ultimate put-down—the closest we could come to calling someone a name (which we were taught not to do) without actually doing so. Reminding our chosen enemies, even subtly, they had a color (and that it was black) served a mean purpose—and a demeaning one.

Mother wit—that old knowledge, held in such regard in my community, is an uncommon sense as well as a common one. It contains the paradox of a self-destructive understanding imposed by race as well as the creative tradition embraced by ethnic identity. The racial dimensions of mother wit forced that mother's parental exchange with her child into a diminishing realm where his creativity, energy, and entitled playfulness are manipulated by her knowledge of how safely he can negotiate his spirit in a society that makes his color matter. This "pitfall of racial reasoning" meant that at the moment of her rebuke, the mindfulness that character-izes the intimacy, sense, and feeling of mother wit was yoked by race instead of enabled by the resonant traditions within her ethnic community.[1] All of us—mother, child, and me—were sobered and silenced by the momentary encounter.

Eth(n)icity: A Tracery of Cultural Work

Codes of Conduct is a meditation that emerges out of the silence of moments that are similar, in their reflective nudge, to the one I experienced in the credit union line. The introspective thoughtfulness these moments provoke guides an ethical con-versation where sense and wit converge to discern a common ground of feeling about issues of ethnicity.

Ironically, the identity of color that mother and le-gions before her have used to restrict and yoke a black child's conduct is also a collaborative cultural affirmation. As this "also" links negative purpose to redemptive communion, it locates the necessary ambiguity within *Codes of Conduct*. In one critical sense, racialized discourse enunciates the mali-cious impact of a language that has articulated, legislated, and enforced policies and processes that have institutionalized themselves by reifying the lie of a biological referent. In this regimented space, race identifies what out of a biologized history of cultural conflict has been rendered true and actual based on a perversion of science.

In this same space, however, there is a tracery of cul-tural work, including language, belief, artistry, custom, and value that has emerged precisely because of the ubiquitous

presence of race in public life. The presence and practice of
the African American community that practices this cultural
work in the United States forces a convergence of memory and
history, practice and process that is both racial and ethnic. It
is a synergy of form and ideology. African American ethnicity
claims what has been forced into reality by the historical
presence of a biologized racial discourse as well as what has
been actualized within society's realms through the reality
that race has constructed. In other words, although race does
not necessarily, immediately, or always claim an ethnic imperative, ethnicity absolutely and completely acknowledges
the complexity that race has configured.

This book explores ethical conduct that either implicitly or explicitly traces the architecture of ethnic identity.
Despite what some may suspect, I have not only chosen
"ethics" to specify this conduct because of the alliterative
appeal of its relationship to ethnicity, though I cannot completely deny the aesthetic pleasure this association of words
brings to me.

Like ethnicity and because of it, ethics too has its
complication. Ethics practices a moral imperative that is
subject to narratives of community and culture. Theological
ethicist Stanley Hauerwas argues a similarly grounded perspective and notes that "questions of what we ought to be
are necessary background for questions of what we ought to
do. . . . Action descriptions gain their intelligibility from
the role they play in a community's history."[2] An ethical
imperative acknowledges its cultural generation when practice and identity formulate actions that have a referential
and expressive relationship to ethnicity—our "community's
history."

These terms, *ethics* and *ethnicity*, collide and collapse as
they encounter each other. In this activity, they generate a

context in which they both acknowledge and avoid the other, becoming an *eth(n)icity* of sorts. The encounter produces what this book argues is a narrative coherence that articulates the way moral imaginations construct behaviors that are intimate with and close to our community's identity as well as to its social, political, and economic histories. As a consequence, the reach of ethics and ethnicity is both diffuse and thick, creative and destructive, affirming and disabling. Within the politics that racism in the United States has created and enforced, ethical conduct has had no choice but to claim its association with ethnic identity. The persistent political objective of the state makes it both the adjudicator and the arbitrator of our ethical conduct.

The ideology of a "United" States apparently argues vigorously that cultural (ethnic) pluralism grounds its very being. However, the state operates by maintaining an authoritative and rigorous cultural silence and by asserting instead the uncomplicated distinction of race as a legislatively condoned difference. Racial difference that is generated, identified, and nurtured by legislative process insufficiently addresses the complex issues of ethnicity that matter within a community. Public policies are racialized; responses to those policies are ethnically inscribed. Social systems are race-coded; reactions to these systems are determined through a filter of ethnicity. Political strategies are race-baited; policies that emerge from these strategies are ensnared within ethnic differences. And so it goes.

The tyranny of a white majority easily asserts itself in the midst of this litany of calls and responses between system and populace. Despite our Whitmanesque delusions of democratic vistas, thin and racially qualified political ideologies challenge the thicker potentials of a communitarian ethic. The antics of the state's corporate policy-making sustain destabilizing inequities and give body and substance to racialized ideologies.

An actual issue of statehood might best illustrate what I indict as the activity of a corporate and bodied racial politic. Consider the effort of the District of Columbia to claim itself as the state of New Columbia. It exists now only as a shadow state. Jesse Jackson serves as its "shadow senator" (a descriptive metaphor whose dark comedic potential I only reluctantly leave behind). New Columbia challenges corporeality because it is not yet made, not in/corporated. However, the late 1993 debate that echoed through the chambers of the House of Representatives regarding the district's corporate (statehood) potential was a racialized and rancid battery of abuses hurled at the bodies of its citizens. Congressional representatives voiced to the House gallery their concerns that residents of the district must learn how to behave as a city before they could behave as a state and expressed their worries that the district's need for prison space would strain the pockets of the wannabe state and its neighbors. Their vitriol and disrespect made it clear that this was not a debate about statehood as much as it was an interrogation of personhood—of humanity. There was a distinctive and familiar hue to their politicized rhetoric. As long as D.C. looks as black as it is, the issue of states' rights veils what the shadow knows is an issue of human rights.

Standing Close to Feeling

The righteousness inherent to a cultural criticism lies within its moral imperative. The ethical territories of this conversation emerge and become apparent as it acknowledges the way in which difference activates and identifies culture. In many ways, issues of difference and culture, and the ethical decisions that reflect their realities, call for common sense. It is relatively easy to anticipate a relationship between culture and conduct. This is, after all, the very stuff of our national identity.

However, I want to problematize, just for a moment, the notion of a common sense in order to better understand the complicated and potentially perplexing formulation that posits a singular, universally accessible knowledge (a.k.a. "a common sense") that actually destabilizes our common ground (the United States) rather than stabilizes it. Problematizing the phrase resists the simplistic essentialism of its most readily accepted definition, one that implicates a kind of ordinary and generalized knowledge. When literary and cultural theorist Edward Said writes of the "sense" of critical consciousness, he directs a complicated acuity toward

> what political, social, and human values are entailed in the reading, production, and transmission of every text. To stand between culture and system therefore is to stand *close to*—closeness itself having a particular value . . . a concrete reality about which political, moral, and social judgments have to be made and, if not only made, then exposed and demystified.[3]

The common sense of cultural work makes feeling particular, intimate, and shared. We stand, as Said suggests, "close to" feeling, assigning "value" to this intimacy and to the work it compels us to do. It challenges the agency of both reader and text. "Common" and shared considerations of equity and balance, and emotive impressions of a "sense" that can and should provoke intimacy and urge feeling emerge as critical to the paradigms of a cultural criticism. It is this associative nexus that is privileged by *Codes of Conduct*.

Political and social processes (like those that inhabit the D.C. statehood debate) limn the boundaries of exclusion and inclusion, and trace the relationship between ethnicity and ethics that this book explores. My configuration of ethnicity as being constitutive but not singularly indicative of race occasions the interdisciplinary discussions within this project and its claim to a wide terrain of interrogation. My terrain is a storytelling space. This is a book of a culture's stories, from literature, public life, and contemporary and historic events. All migrate, textu(r)ally, across a space widened and articulated both by my intellectual and my personal histories.

One consequence of this migration is that this book uses "our" a lot. The simplest way to clarify this referentiality is to explain that I mean both you, the reader, and me, the author. It also indicates that my own identity is unambiguously located within the African American community that is the subject of my reflections. My pronominal claim in this narrative style allows me to place myself within all these communities, virtual and imagined, and to claim the knowledge, the experience, the passion and the responsibility of each of them. However, when my editor asked the question that this narrative performance begs: "Are you sometimes hiding behind the 'our?' " my quick response acknowledged the thin veneer her insight pierced. "Nope," I replied. "Always."

Upon reflection however, I am indeed behind this "our," but I am not veiled. Both from need and through style I am within and without this text. The access I claim to the spaces of narrative control as their author, and the interstices of narrative context I inhabit as its subject are reflected in the constant return, within the text of *Codes of Conduct* to a theme of the struggle that exists between public and private domains. They sift me within, without, and between their various territories. Biblical scholar Renita Weems argues this as a perspective specific to African American women who have "insisted upon holding in creative tension her African American and female identities simultaneously, her history overwhelmingly [encourages] her to hold in tandem all of the components of her identity."[4] I understand, intimately, both the creativity and the tension that Weems references. My life stories and those from fiction, historical and political practice, aesthetic expression, public life, and popular cultures all locate themselves within a common ground of African American ethnicity. There I, those I love, and those whose traditions I value and validate as I struggle through my days, reside. So my process and my plan in *Codes of Conduct* have been to create a means through which this textu(r)al collage is made somewhat visible.

Philosopher and theologian Cornel West elegantly framed what I value within this industry of cultural criticism in a PBS interview with Bill Moyers. West argued that "the quest for truth, the quest for the good, the quest for the beautiful, for me, presupposes allowing the suffering to speak, allowing victims to be visible, and allowing social misery to be put on the agenda of those with power."[5]

In three main chapters—"The Body Politic," "Language, Thought, and Culture," and "The Moral Lives of Children"—I attend to the sounds of oppositional discourse and I visualize the embodied result of race and ethnicity as they are negotiated in realms of power. These chapters—on black women and the visual power of the black and female body; on language that has aesthetic resonance and racialized drama; and on our children's challenged habits of surviving—question the narrative effect, in the stories of African American community life, of citizenship that is meted out sparingly when one's ethnicity is colored.[6]

CHAPTER ONE

The Body Politic

There was no respect or wonder for her silence.
　　　　—Patricia Williams writing about Tawana Brawley
　　in *The Alchemy of Race and Rights*

"No wonder," she said at last, "no wonder. . . . Look at
how I look."
　　　　—Toni Morrison, *Song of Solomon*

We have no patterns for relating across our human
differences as equals. As a result, those differences have
been misnamed and misused.
　　　　—Audre Lorde, *Sister Outsider*

My grandmother warned me away from red. I thought about this, when I watched Anita Hill's appearance before the United States Senate Judiciary Committee. She wore a teal blue suit with a modest row of military-like double buttons down the front. Her family sat supportively arrayed behind her. As she introduced them—proudly pausing to note her parents' upcoming anniversary—naming cousins and other kin, the event seemed like anything but what it was: the beginning moments of her testimony against (then) President George Bush's nominee for the United States Supreme Court.

My grandmother was right, nice girls did not wear red, I thought—and Professor Hill had clearly been raised as a nice girl. She was very properly mannered, neatly attired, softly spoken, and in every dimension certainly a "credit to the race." Professor Hill was clearly what my grandmother had in mind when she encouraged me and my sisters to carry ourselves well, to speak with precision and care, and to bring honor to our families. However, although all of the same behavioral codes from my private, family-centered education were being remarkably emulated in Professor Hill's polite demeanor, the occasion was nonetheless a serious challenge to the weightier directives I had been urged to follow in public situations. For all of the frank talk about sexual harassment, pubic hair, and pornography, Professor Hill may as well have worn red.

My grandmother's admonition was a part of her

ongoing lecture series to me and my sisters on morality, values, and proper conduct for young Negro girls. I remember the color lecture (wearing red, having dark skin) and the peach speech best.

The peach speech happened in the summer. We were in Eastern Market in Detroit—a large open air market that began our summer Saturday mornings and that my older sister Karen and I called Easter market. I was trying to pick out free stone instead of cling peaches and Grandmother Celia decided it would be a perfect time to give me and Karen the fuzz lecture. She had us "handle" a peach—passing it back and forth between us, rubbing it smooth and clear of its soft fuzz until the contrast between ours and the one she still held was evident. That, Grandmother said, is the difference between a nice girl and one that has been passed around. If we put the one we had passed between us back with the others, no one would choose the well-handled peach over the fresh ones. Karen and I looked. It was absolutely apparent which peach had been passed around. We shook our heads, agreeing with our grandmother. Then we went home and made cobbler.

Grandmother's other lesson, the one about red, had no touchable peach-like text. And there was no reward in pies. It was simply that nice girls do not wear red. And especially nice girls that are dark, like you Karla Francesca (my grandmother always called me by my two names). She eyed me over her coverlets where she lay in the front bedroom. It makes you look common.

Looking common was the ultimate sin in my grandmother's eyes. One of the reasons we had to polish our already white sneakers and shoe laces with white Kiwi polish until they looked "immaculate" was so that we would not look common. I learned that word, immaculate, long before I should have. I am sure I knew it as a preschooler although, if asked, I would probably have said it has something to do with sneakers. But unpolished shoes, ashy elbows and knees, and red dresses could all lead to the same unalterable state—looking common.

I have carried grandmother's warnings with me for many years. Sometimes, when teaching an American literature class T. S. Eliot's poem "The Love Song of J. Alfred Prufrock," I tell them her peach story when we come to the line "Do I dare to eat a peach?" My class mostly laughs at the old-fashioned idea of virtue my grandmother's story advances. But some of them look reflective, struck by the decided contrast between fuzzy and de-fuzzed peaches. In the same way that her peach story recurs for me at what seem to be incongruous moments, her warning about red, connected as it is to her lessons in comportment, has fixed itself in my memory.

Although I do wear red these days, I am very aware, each time I do, the statement I am making. I am not sure yet whether I am talking (inwardly) to myself (you are still a nice girl Karla Francesca and this red dress looks good on your dark self); whether I am talking back to my grandmother (but nice girls would not talk back to their elders); or whether I am talking outwardly to whoever sees me and shares my subliminal red nag. Is it the public imagery that I challenge, or the private memory? I am still conflicted about the intersection between public and private, and ever aware of the subtext of my grandmother's intimate awareness about public bodies—dark skinned, daringly colored, and female. I find myself anticipating events where "credit to the race" women will appear with an embarrassingly superficial but difficult-to-repress interest in what they will wear. So, when Anita Hill was scheduled to appear before the Senate committee, and as I waited in front of my television for that appearance, part of me was waiting to see what she would wear. I knew for a fact that it would not be red.

The event of the Senate hearings compromised both of the things Professor Hill was supposed to keep quiet: her sexuality and her color. It could be argued that the issues of her body and Supreme Court nominee Clarence Thomas's that were made public during those days of the Senate hearings were signs of the times—a contemporary nod to the liberated social politics of the late twentieth century. However, I think they were actually indications of the reappearance of the same old events and biases that made my grandmother's mid-century warning to me inevitable.

Since that fall when Anita Hill gave her testimony, I have thought a great deal about public appearances, black women, bodies, and sexuality. "Testimonial" itself has a con-flicted etymology for women coming, as it does, from the Latin root for testicles.[1] This incident of linguistic source and history is not as innocuous as it may seem. The colonizing habit of linguistic dominance is not only an event that dis-places and replaces geographic territories; it is a matter of the displacement of psychical and spiritual territory as well. In other words, the reterritorializing history of slavery and domi-nance that displaced a nation of black bodies must be under-stood as a displacement that was facilitated through a series of distancing behaviors away from motherland and away from mothertongue. The ideological ambiguities that are imposed by our everyday uses of language are complicated in narra-tives that recall the histories of colonialism and slavery in their recitation or in the voice and body of the speaker. Anita Hill's situation was especially vulnerable. As a lawyer, she was accustomed to making the narrow specificity of legal language work to displace ambiguity. However, her culture and her body's experience within the history of the United

States both intersected and dissected the frames of U.S. English, making the conflict between it and her untenable and vulnerable. Senators' questions to her underscored this conflict. Did you write it down (Thomas's abusive words and the harassing events)? Did you keep a journal? They asked these questions innocently, as if journal records or diary entries kept by women ever held any sway in American literary history.

The experience of exile makes one question the sanctuaries that "learning the language and the culture" seem to promise upon assimilation. Kenyan writer Ngugi wa Thiong'o, who dealt with the psychic exile of colonial language by rejecting it, has suggested that language holds the soul prisoner. Surely the October 1991 Senate hearings made visible the bars of a spiritual prison.

Involuntary migration must be understood differently from the voluntary immigration of European (for example) communities into the United States. In this light, Anita Hill's appearance in the chambers of Congress captures the visual and spoken dimension of a testimony of exile. Despite her personal, individual, and dramatically successful integration into U.S. academe and what seem to be upper-class sanctuaries, the inquisition of her body and the interrogation of her words demonstrated the displaced subjectivity of an altered state of black identity. These identities contradict the perceived icons that U.S. histories constantly display as the text of its national identity (the Statue of Liberty, the words of Emma Lazarus beneath the statue, "Give me your tired, your poor. . . ."). Black women's bodies have a history of reductive and voyeuristic encounters with jurisprudence that diminish our intellects, ignore our character, and challenge the fairness doctrine that allegedly motivates our political and legal structures. These moments disable the individual ethic that Anita Hill thought she could command, which is, if you do the right thing, if you stay out of trouble, if you get an education, you can make it in America. Journalist Ellis Cose explores this dilemma in *The Rage of the Privileged Class.* Cose writes that "again and again I spoke with blacks who have every accoutrement of success. I heard a plaintive declaration followed by various versions of an unchanging and urgently put question. 'I have done everything I was supposed to do. I have stayed out of trouble with the law, gone to the right schools, and worked myself nearly to death. *What more do they want?* . . . Why in God's name won't they accept me as a full human being?' "[2]

Hill's personal history of integrity and competence, her familial support, and her singular success should have commanded the respectful space allotted to Clarence Thomas. His testimony inscribed a territory where his accomplishments indicated a personal triumph amidst a difficult environment. Here, however, testimony honored its linguistic roots. His male black body was allowed, even encouraged to show his "balls." Toni Morrison's consideration of this embodied moment leads to this conclusion:

> What would have been extraordinary would have been to ignore Thomas's body, for in ignoring it, the articles [news reports on his nomination] would have had to discuss in some detail that aspect of him more difficult to appraise—his mind. . . . It seems blazingly clear that with this unprecedented opportunity to hover over and to cluck at, to meditate and ponder the limits and excesses of black bodies, no other strategies were going to be entertained.[3]

This does not mean that blackness was not a handicap here; but the benefit of maleness weighted the event against Hill.

It was, after all, a time for "testimony" and etymologically, at least, she did not have any.

In an important acknowledgment of my grandmother's conservatism, the ethics my grandmother encouraged in her grandgirls followed her well-considered reflection on the history of gendered ethnic stereotype and abuse in U.S. history and her determination about what could save us from the abuse that accompanies stereotype. When she warned us away from red, she reinforced the persistent historical reality that black women's bodies are a site of public negotiation and private loss.

The reflections that center this chapter recall historic, literary, and contemporary black women whose bodies speak more powerfully than their minds to women and men whose ethnicities are different from theirs, whose color stereotypes their character within their culture, and whose class distinguishes their potentials. Each representation and response indicates how vigorously the public display controls the private image—adhering to the representation as persistently as my grandmother's red warning attaches itself to my memories of her.

Now We See . . . Face to Face

Despite the fact that two hundred years had passed, there was precedent for Professor Anita Hill's 1991 testimony before the skeptical senators on the United States Senate Judiciary Committee. And although Phillis Wheatley was only a teenager when she sat in a New England courthouse in 1772 before her Boston jury, there are parallels in the two events— visual as well as contextual—that encourage a comparison between them.

Professor Anita Hill begins her testimony before the Senate Judiciary Committee on October 11, 1991. AP/Wide World Photos

Poet Phillis Wheatley, frontispiece from the 1773 edition of Poems on
Various Subjects, Religious and Moral.

I was a youngster when my mother told me about a Senegalese girl, held captive in colonial America, who became a poet. Mother may not have known the courthouse story about Phillis Wheatley, but she told me about her cruel capture and together we imagined her frightening journey to America in the hold of a slave ship. Separated forever from her family, her name lost to childhood memory, she was sold into slavery in the New England household of John Wheatley. Phillis Wheatley's poem "On Being Brought from Africa to America" was one of the first I learned by heart. I felt connected to her artistry and passion, and the tragedy of her personal history brought me to tears. Her story appealed to my dramatic notions of the way the world worked. I had, after all, been engrossed in captivity stories for a good chunk of my elementary school years. Mostly, these were stories of white women captured by Indians who, fascinated with their golden haired, corn-tassel-like beauty, incorporated these pitiful and innocent pioneer women into their lives. These women lived in goddess-like splendor until a white soldier-colonist rescued them just before they came of sexual age and carried them triumphantly back to the civilized colonial world.

I think my mother must have grown weary of my captivation with these captivity narratives, and that was when, and why, she told me Phillis's story. No one ever rescued Wheatley from the hands of her colonial kidnappers. And she was to die, abandoned, penniless, and suffering from malnutrition, in a New England poorhouse. However, between the time of her eighth year (when she was enslaved) and her forty-first year (when she died), Wheatley became a poet.

Colonial America did not easily accept that one whose color condemned both her humanity and her potential could write elegant verse in the style of the British poets who were their literary models and heroes. So before Wheatley was able to publish in America, the contradiction between her color and her competence had to be addressed. Someone decided that a judicial-like examination would be the best forum for this interrogation. It was clearly not merely an educational issue—if it had been, the exam could have been held in a school building's classroom. But Wheatley's literary talent strained against and threatened the reason of the codes of judicial conduct that kept black and white lives separate. Her moment of public examination foreshadowed the cruel circle of justice that was to ensnare Anita Hill nearly two centuries later.

Eighteen white men—churchmen, politicians, merchants, the governor and lieutenant governor among them—gathered for Wheatley's examination. They described themselves as being among the "best judges" to determine whether Phillis Wheatley, who was, in their estimation, "brought an uncultivated Barbarian from Africa" was able to write the poetry she insisted was her own composition.[4] They met in a New England courthouse. Because a federal green cloth was an ordinary draping for the colonial courtroom tables of eighteenth-century New England, it is likely that such a piece of fabric separated the seventeen-year-old Phillis from her panel of judges. The circumstances of Wheatley's hearing make it likely that her questioners expressed disbelief and skepticism during her interrogation. I believe it as likely that disrespect, in tone and manner, may well have accompanied the questioning. The event's occasion was certainly disrespectful. Thomas Hutchinson, the governor of the Boston colony, led the inquisition of the "young Negro girl" who claimed authorship of a thin edition of poems. The British edition, already published in that country, claimed on the frontispiece that they had been "written by herself." After what had to be a serious and sustained examination, "some of the best judges" would finally attest that she was indeed the source of the words in her book.

Two centuries later, Professor of Law Anita Hill would also find herself nearly encircled by a panel of white males who would listen to her claim the legitimacy of her words. A legislative chamber was the gathering place for Hill's testimony, as it had been for Wheatley's, and a federal green cloth, reminiscent of colonial courthouses, separated her from her adjudicators.

The paralegal setting of Hill's testimony highlighted the question of the day—was she telling the truth about Judge Clarence Thomas, President Bush's nominee to fill a Supreme Court vacancy. Like Phillis Wheatley who claimed the legitimacy of her words, Hill's testimony before the gathering of senators who would decide on Thomas's candidacy was designed to verify her language—the words she had submitted on a sworn affidavit and the experiences those words described. Hill stoically faced the senators' skepticism, outright disbelief, and derision. The presumptive austerity of the hearing degenerated quickly as the senators took turns abusing Hill's character and challenging her intellect. I have no difficulty imagining Wheatley's experience in the 1772 hearings as a similar emotional wasting. Any private identity Anita Hill had prior to those hearings would be reinvented by the public rehearsal of her testimony and the senators' public and political posturing.[5]

In both cases, words seem to center the conflict of credibility, scripting a rhetorical parallelism that ensnares both events. Anita Hill's claim of sexual harassment was certainly different in kind, but not in degree, from Phillis Wheatley's claim to authorship. Both women's testimonies were labeled incredible and both attempted a negotiation of racial and gender politics within which neither had a stable or legitimized presence. The legitimacy of their testimony was determined in a court of public and political opinion that had already judged the likelihood of their credibility to be in large measure associated with their gender and their ethnicity. In a fair forum, the external evidence confronting the judiciary—their female bodies and their African color—would have been absolutely irrelevant, but because of the specifically racist and sexist history of cultural politics in the United States, both were absolutely essential factors and clearly relevant to each woman's credibility in those deliberations.

Both events led to a crisis of identity within the body politic. White males held titular power and control over these hearings. How they thought about and how they behaved toward black women enforced (and created) the cultural politics of their eras. These judicial bodies behaved in a manner consistent with the ethical codes of jurisprudence, which call for a blind justice, unaffected by privately held notions of their culturally invested superiority. However, the conflict of representation that the black and female bodies would initiate challenged the notions of judicial restraint. The ethical determinations that the Senate panel was gathered to debate hinged directly upon the ethnicity of those who testified before it.[6] The ethical quandary that Wheatley and Hill placed on their examiners challenged the ability of the examiners to visualize the claims and words of the two women apart from their ethnicities. These panels had to judge in a color-blind way and had to render at once the identities of Wheatley and Hill as invisible and their claims as visible. The 1772 jury admitted by its presence that the only reason they had gathered was because Phillis Wheatley was an African woman. The 1991 jury may as well have confessed the same.

Even though Hill's and Wheatley's words seem to occupy the central position in the events that brought them before their judicial bodies, the more visually powerful display of their bodies displaced the authoritative claims of language. The sworn affidavit and the volume of poetry—the texts of both events—behaved in similar ways. Both were scripts brought to the forum of oracy. However, both forums were intrinsically conflicted sites because this particular language came from black women and theirs were the very bodies that political and legal systems in the United States have worked hard to render passive and silent. In other words, when Hill and Wheatley spoke, their black bodies immediately became key to how their testimony would be received. Within the chambers of legislative authority, where ideologies of both statehood and nationhood are preserved, and ideologies of personhood are determined, these dark and female bodies challenged the juridical authority of the state. Even if the territorial integrity of New England saved Phillis Wheatley from southern slavery, this geographical border did not resist the powerful visual of her body's politics. It was enough to contradict what she said she had done. And even if a lawyer's license and professorial tenure placed Anita Hill into the ranks of the nation's intellectual elites, they did not supersede her blackness and femaleness. The state assaulted both Wheatley's and Hill's personhood far beyond its power to salvage or legitimate their words. Legitimacy was not the legacy of this encounter with the state. Instead, it was its antagonistic provocateur.

I move back and forth between these incidents—one reconstructed from historical and literary record, the other preserved for posterity on C-SPAN videotape. Although there are dramatic differences between the two, not to mention the gulf of centuries, something keeps pulling them back together for me. And it is more than the visual politics of two black women facing a semi-circle of disbelieving white males. What draws me back, again and again, to these women, are the numbers of encounters I can add to theirs that challenge the same stereotypes, that reenact the same emotional dramas, and that display the same reductive politics. I have even imagined Hill and Wheatley in a room talking to each other about their experiences—exchanging identical words, recalling like responses, and reliving together their discomfort. In my reverie, their words blend together until it is difficult to tell one from the other. If I were looking into a mirror's image, the consistency of their reflection could not be more stunning.

If Hill and Wheatley could face each other, we might imagine their interaction as a mirrored contemplation. The intriguing self-reflective potential within their mutual gaze encourages my speculation on the relationship between private identities (a poet and a law professor) and public deconstructions of those identities (a black woman and a black woman). A mirrored image encourages confrontation with the racialized and sexualized realities of American cultural history. Absent the mirror, events might successfully insist that they are discrete episodes and really only about the agendas that allegedly motivated the encounters. Did Wheatley write the book? Did Hill tell the truth? But this isn't what these events are about at all. Instead, looking through the mirror we see the image that controls the text. Did a black girl write the book? Did an African American woman tell the truth? The visual image makes it clear that these encounters are neither socially nor politically blind. The lesson lies in our response to situations like this one. If black women behave as if race and sex are peripheral rather than central, we participate in these encounters at considerable risk. If, however, we name the event for what it is, then those who undertake behaviors that engage the stereotype rather than our intellects do so at considerable risk to themselves. In *Black Ice*, Lorene Cary recalls those situations when black women, weary of the abuse of stereotype, find it necessary to "turn it out."[7]

> My mother and her mother, who had worked in a factory, and her mother, who had cleaned apartments in Manhattan, had been studying these people all their lives. . . . And I had studied them. I had studied my mother as she turned out elementary schools and department stores.
>
> I always saw it coming. Some white department-store manager would look at my mother and see no more than a modestly dressed young black woman making a tiresome complaint. He'd use that tone of voice they used when they had *important* work elsewhere. Uh-oh. Then he'd dismiss her with his eyes. I'd feel her body stiffen next to me, and I'd know that he'd set her off. . . .
>
> And then it began in earnest, the turning out. She never moved back. It didn't matter how many people were in line. It didn't matter how many telephones were ringing. . . . Sometimes she'd talk through her teeth, her lips moving double time to bite out the consonants. Then she'd get personal. . . .
>
> Turning out, I learned, was not a matter of style; cold indignation worked as well as hot fury. Turning out had to do with will. I came to regard my mother's will as a force of nature, an example of . . . black power and black duty. (58–59)

When my book club—a group of African American women with the signifying name "The Friday Night

Women"—read *Black Ice*, "J." asked if we ever had to "turn it out." The tenor of the night's discussion changed as we alternately shared the hilarity of the moments when we just decided to go on and "act colored" as some of us called it, and we also relived the pain of us all having had that same experience. In one sense, turning it out or acting colored means that we give up trying to respond to a situation as if both we and they (white people and/or men) are operating within the same codes of conduct. It can mean handing over to our adversary our version of the stereotype that motivates their disrespect to us—just to prove to them that they could no better handle the stereotype than they can determine and control our character. No one wins in that situation, but usually we feel better. The events we shared among ourselves all had a similar trigger—it was when someone, a child's school principal or teacher, a store clerk, medical personnel, had treated us as if we had no sense of our own, no ability to filter through whatever nonsense they were feeding us, or no earned, adult power to make choices in our children's lives. We were treated as if we were not grown women, as if we had no mind or character, no common sense or personal integrity, and no basic, fundamental understanding of fairness. We were treated as if we were nothing but an inept and passive black body.

　　I recall an early teaching experience in Michigan, when I was teaching a composition class made up of students from various majors across the university. That section had a large number of nursing students enrolled. One night they brought me their medical textbook and shared with me the chapter on patient care and intervention in emergency room medicine. The book stated quite explicitly that if your emergency room patient was a black woman, medical personnel could expect her to be overweight, wearing a wig (so make certain you remove it before care), screaming and hysterical beyond a "reasonable" measure of her pain and discomfort, and very likely to be suffering from pelvic inflammatory disease. This diagnosis, regimen for care, and prediction of patient behavior would be based only on the patient's gender and ethnicity!

Sharing that memory with the Friday Night Women occasioned more than one story about our own medical nightmares and the disrespect we earn simply by walking into a white physician's office or find ourselves needing emergency care. One of my closest friends has a brother who is an obstetrician-gynecologist. She has learned from him the deep level of disrespect black women experience who come to an emergency room with pain in their lower abdominal region. There is a medical term acronym—P.I.D., for pelvic inflammatory disease—that is called, in-house, "pussy-in-distress," especially when black women are so afflicted. If a black woman presents with abdominal pain, this infection is often the first suspected because of its association, in medical circles, with sexual activity. It is easy to see, given such anecdotal evidence, why our black and female bodies incite such disrespect, especially when illness makes us vulnerable and renders us (sometimes) silent.

My own frequent and severe episodes with asthma have often forced me into emergency room care. I've had physicians tell me to just get a good cough syrup and go home, call me "honey" and "sweetheart," use my first name (a familiarity that is earned, not assumed, in my community), or question my record of the medicines I take, sure that I cannot know the dosage of the solumedrol (an anti-inflammatory steroid) injection I need to pull me out of the episode. Now I carry a physician's letter with me, explaining my history and emergency care needs in case I cannot get to her in time for treatment. It is a step I know I need to take because too many physicians have read the same textbook my Michigan students were taught from. Asthma, unfortunately, keeps me from "turning it out"—it is hard to turn it out when you cannot even breathe. I have, however, experienced some measure of retribution when I had to make an emergency room visit during a family reunion. My younger sister, who is a physician, accompanied me to the hospital. Leslie can be subtle, and she waited just long enough through the paternalistic nonsense that was keeping me from getting immediate and intelligent treatment until she let them know she was a doctor, and then proceeded to "turn it out."

Leslie and I have had some of our most cathartic moments when we have "turned it out" together. One Christmas Eve, we were accused of shoplifting because a store clerk had left a magnetic sensor in a pair of gloves we had purchased. Somehow, the receipt imprinted with ISOTONER GLVS and the price was not enough to satisfy the store detective. So after intelligence, evidence, politeness, reason, and tolerance did not work, we decided to make him sorry he had ever stopped these two sisters on a snowy Christmas Eve while we were trying to get home so we could go to church and where is your manager and the clerk who subjected us to this abuse and no we're not going anywhere you bring them here to us and obviously you cannot be in charge because you don't have enough sense so bring me the president of the store and call my lawyer and write your name and your mama's name down right here and who hired you into this position, we want their name too.

Leslie and I chose to confront that white store detective with what he saw. We acknowledged the persuasive visual power of our black bodies and took control of that image. Sometimes, though, African American women do not recognize the mirror as a part of our realities. And we do not disable its power with our awareness of it. I believe that knowing what others may imagine they see when they look at us is necessary and critical information. Without this awareness, we behave as if our bodies and our color do not provoke a certain stereotype and initiate a particular response. And we turn over to others, who do not have our best interests at heart, the power of the image.

It is important to realize the potential of the mirror to both reveal and distort. If we have recognized the control it would exert over how others treat us, the mirrored image is revelatory. If, however, the mirror operates without our intervention, it powerfully distorts our appearances and gains a dangerous control. This contradictory and conflicting imagery duplicates the trauma imposed by racism and sexism. The shifty gaze of these prejudices, as they target blackness or femaleness or both, often has a tragically disfiguring assault. Blackwomen's black and female bodies complicate the reductive visual stereotypes of prejudice, challenging its simplemindedness. Blackwomen's bodies visually assault the systems designed to neatly and easily identify the unempowered. Sexism alone targets women. Racism's targets are the ethnic other. Blackwomen deconstruct the formal stability of those prejudices and challenge the politically and socially legislated impermeability of those boundaries.

As varied as our stories are, it seems that at some point African American women are forced into a confrontation with the confounding physical reality our bodies represent. This moment of facing is so critical to our psyches, and so frequently rehearsed in our everyday lives, that unless we have a response (like "turning it out") ritualized into the patterns of our daily lives, we are likely to find ourselves as underprepared as bell hooks charged Anita Hill with being. In

Black Looks: Race and Representation, hooks challenges Hill's lack of preparation for the "context of white supremacist capitalist patriarchy" that structured the hearings.[8] Her lack of response to the provocations that challenged her identity, hooks argues, could only be the unresponsiveness of someone whose faith in a system "that has rarely worked for women" is unchallenged and misguided.

> Anita Hill stated her case. She did not appear to have a strategy that was based on considering the needs, desires, and expectations of her audience, both that of the Senate committee or the millions of viewers watching her. . . . Had Anita Hill been an advocate of feminism, mild or militant, she would have brought to the hearings the kind of feminist thinking and awareness that would have enabled her to face the reality that white supremacist patriarchy had already chosen Thomas. It would have given her the wisdom to understand that to challenge that choice . . . she would need to subvert the system. Subversion requires strategy. Simply stating the case was not enough. . . .
>
> In such a context, it is not surprising that Anita Hill became the object of fierce, sexist interrogation. To many viewers, her calm demeanor was a sign of her integrity, that she had chosen the high moral ground. Yet to some of us, it was yet another example of black female stoicism in the face of sexist/racist abuse. While it may not have changed the outcome of the hearings in any way, had Hill been more strategic and passionate, and dare I say it, even angry at the assault on her character, it would have made the hearings less an assault on the psyches of black females watching.[9]

I would add that Hill's own psyche may well have benefited from the passion.

Regardless of our stature within our communities, our incomes, or our schooling, there comes some essential moment when black women must acknowledge the powerful impact of our physical appearance. How we look is a factor in what happens to us. Whether our conduct controls for this factor, or if it ignores it, has a potential consequence on its outcome. I think the reality of racism and sexism means that we must configure our private realities to include an awareness of what our public image might mean to others. This is not paranoia. It is preparedness. If we are healthy and strong, this figurative moment may make it necessary that we "turn it out." If we are battle-weary and spiritually weakened, it may cause us to feel depressed and powerless. Ideally, it is a knowledge that allows us to gain strength of character and energy to do aggressive and passionate battle with racism and prejudice.

Whatever our responses, when we see ourselves—our bodies—as others see us, the confrontational gaze is both dark and clear. In African American literature by women, a mirrored encounter often figuratively represents this moment of facing, bringing both resonance and tone to the scriptural passage "Now we see as through a glass, darkly; but then face to face."

Look at How I Look

In Toni Morrison's *Song of Solomon*, Hagar's moment of body-discovery throws her into a panic of frenzied and pitiful shopping to correct the image she understands to be the barrier to her cousin Milkman's love.[10] Her grandmother has bought her a compact, and "Hagar saw a tiny bit of her face reflected in the mirror" (312). She took the compact then and stared into the mirror for a long while. 'No wonder,' she said at last. . . . No wonder. . . . Look at how I look" (312). Hagar's determination to change the image her lover sees translates into a palpable anguish as she moves from store to store in a frenetic search that "could not let go until the energy and busyness culminated a beauty that would dazzle him." At home, she strips herself naked, garnishes herself with every brand-name commodity imaginable, and covers her face with "sunny glow," "mango tango," and "baby clear sky light." Ultimately, Hagar is forced to the realization that her enterprise will not effect the change she feels is essential. Her melancholy over this discovery eventually destroys her and it happens that death is the only silence that Hagar can bear.

Now, a harsh comparison may see this as an ultimate "shop-'til-you-drop" episode; however, I think it more important to indicate how poorly Hagar understands Milkman's superficiality and how much power she gives him when she falls victim to his image of her—one that enables her own vulnerability. Milkman's sight was no different from Guitar's ("He looked at her again. Pretty. Pretty little black girl. Pretty little black-skinned girl" [310]). Had she then resisted the one-dimensional stereotype that his gaze favored, the glimpse in her mirror would have been a revelatory and enabling moment. It might have been more like "Look what that fool is missing." Instead, his persuasive and diminished ethics distort the reality of her character and conduct, asserting itself over her spirit, and compromising her vulnerability. Because Hagar chooses to attend to the image rather than the reality, her only moment of real action—the frenzied search through the stores for the right look—is an essentially self-destructive behavior. Her telling glimpse in the mirror becomes a fateful glance.

Sometimes, without the well of strength from which Lorene Cary draws, and from which my grandmother's warning was crafted, the mirrored image distorts reality rather than clarifies it. If our psyches are not strong-willed, if we have been so abused by prejudice and meanness that we do not see clearly, we might enable an image that damages us rather than disempowers them. This is what happened to Hagar. Milkman's abusive treatment distorted her vision. Similarly, the dangerous and diminishing cultural politics of our times may be a powerful filter across our mirrors.

Some configuration of the body politic's culturally enforced stereotypes appears in fiction and in nonfiction both, situating our bodies as the one factor that continues to mediate intertextually between our artistry and our livelihoods. These stereotypes rehearse the narrative codes through which our cultures conduct their business. Unless we are involved in these codes as agents rather than respondents, the brutal and reductive ethic that our ethnicity can provoke is likely to make us victims.

In a contemporary literature that is often discussed critically in terms of the crisis of psychological and/or spiritual identity, the essential feature in this struggle is actually quite superficial. It is our bodies, not our selves. The tragic loneliness blackwomen consistently face as we stand before judgmental others—sometimes white, but sometimes black; sometimes male, but sometimes female—demands that we have some wisdom, experience, and some passion with which to combat this abuse.

Words like Wheatley's and Hill's, and episodes like Morrison's Hagar's can either circumvent or engage the body's narrative. The Friday Night Women had a shared response to Anita Hill's second round of questioning before the Senate committee. We felt that at that point, when the inane questions about her fantasy life, mental stability, and color complexes ruled the discourse, she had exhausted whatever respect the Judiciary Committee was even slightingly due. And although all of us felt similarly disgusted with the antics of John Doggett, who testified against Hill's credibility, his demeanor toward the Senate panel better matched the realpolitik of the event. Failing to give them even superficial respect, Doggett disarmed the panel of their presumed places of honor and spoke back to them in the same obsequious manner with which they spoke to him. Although I do appreciate and honor the effort of Hill's controlled demeanor, the senators took such violent advantage of her quiet and respectful conduct that somebody needed to "turn it out."

Sometimes speech events do illustrate the visual. They allow us to respond to the images our black and female bodies reconstruct naming the abuse—"calling out" the text of racism before it does damage. In these encounters, the conduct of the narrative shifts as a speaking black voice comes to an empowered awareness of the body it sees reflected that is either in or out of her control.

In Gloria Naylor's *Linden Hills*, Willa Nedeed, an abused wife and much maligned woman, struggles desperately to recover the spirit her husband Luther has so drastically damaged.[11] Alleging her infidelity, Luther has imprisoned her in the basement. Living there so long in the dark, deprived of both light and sense, she can no longer trust her touch.

> . . . she reached her hand up and began to touch her own face, her fingers running tentatively across the cheeks and mouth. . . . She tried to place the curves and planes, the shape of the jutting cheekbones and texture of her hair. . . . But it was difficult to keep it all in position. When she returned with the curve of

her ear, the chin had shifted and melted up toward the mouth; the nose dissolved before she could bring back the lips. (267)

Frustrated, "she . . . closed her eyes and used both hands, *trying to form a mirror* between her fingers, the darkness, and memory—but she needed to be sure." Willa finally improvises a mirror using the shiny surface of an aluminum pot. "Holding the pot as still as she could, she found that an image would form . . . a dim silhouette. Rimmed by light, there was the outline of her hair, the shape of the chin . . . the profile of her nose and lips. . . . No doubt remained—she was there (emphasis added; 267–268). Once she was sure, "now that she had actually seen and accepted reality . . . she could rebuild" (268). Willa needed to verify that the woman she knew once existed, still did exist. Her face, whole and viable in the mirror, confirmed her body's reality for her. Finally, her strength and seriousness of purpose superimposed themselves over Luther's evil antics.

Legal scholar Patricia Williams must have an intimate understanding of Willa Nedeed's fear of dismemberment. Gloria Naylor's imaginative rendering of Willa's fear of fracture and invisibility, cited in the section above from *Linden Hills*, is echoed in Williams's words from *The Alchemy of Race and Rights*:

> There are moments in my life when I feel as though a part of me is missing. Those are the times when my skin becomes gummy as clay and my nose slides around on my face and my eyes drip down to my chin. I have to close my eyes at such times and remember myself . . . When all else fails, I reach for a mirror and stare myself down until the features reassemble themselves. [12]

Psychoanalytic philosopher Jacques Lacan argues that dreaming during especially stressful times makes manifest a fragmented body—what he labels as a "fragilization."[13] However, Patricia Williams's episode is not a dream. It's a daytime reality. For black women, the everyday reality of that kind of stress reenacts the dismembering nature of racism and sexism. If we do not take immediate control of that image—staring our own selves down until we reassemble our spirits—we risk the fracture that characterizes so much of the psychic conflict within fiction by black women writers and that is so persistent an aspect of our daily experiences.

Williams's book layers event upon event that asserts her self into the already powerful discourse of racialized and sexualized body politics. In one instance, she hisses a rebuke to a gang of white male athletes who jostle and push her off of what should have been their common ground (a sidewalk)— "Don't I exist for you? See me! And deflect, godammit!" Her reprimand allowed her to "pursue her way, *manumitted back into silence*" (emphasis added).[14] The intentional allusion to manumission in Williams's description recalls the legislative redundancy of women's rights in the United States.

Our bodies—black and female—have historically constituted both implicit and explicit contracts within our legal, political, and cultural systems. Our vocal constraint has complicated the tension that comes from the enforced silence of these contracted identities. In *The Color Purple*, Alice Walker's Celie is told up front, on page one, in the first line and in italics: "*You better not never tell nobody but God.*"[15] Celie is being warned not to tell of the abuse, rape, and trauma that have become the tenor and tone of her daily life. Williams reminds her reader that commercial transactions work in similarly confining ways, constraining "the lively involvement of [contractual] signatories by positioning enforcement

in such a way that parties find themselves in a passive relationship to a document" (224).

The documented positions of the black and female
body in literature and in contemporary cultural politics reinforce notions of constraint and the conflicted nature of our
silence. Even some who believed Anita Hill's testimony
found her guilty of speech. She should have kept quiet, they
argued, rather than tell on a black man and fracture the
fragile nature of the unity of the African American community. Similar allegations met Robin Givens and Desiree
Washington—both victims of fighter Mike Tyson's explosive
violence and both accused of having some motive other than
truth-telling in their public recitations of his abuse.

Robin Givens, Tyson's ex-wife, told about her abuse
on prime time television to Barbara Walters and however
many millions of Americans were watching the interview.
While Givens spoke about his violence, Tyson sat beside her
in absolute silence. Givens chose a public occasion for the
telling, a choice I am certain was well-considered. Desiree
Washington, who accused Tyson of the rape for which he was
convicted, also brought her abuse into a public forum. She
made certain that it was his body, not hers, that must face a
public confrontation. On the other hand, Tawana Brawley,
the fifteen-year-old black girl who was found nearly naked,
streaked with feces, burned, and otherwise brutally abused,
has never spoken out about her trauma. The price of her
silence has been a conspiracy of criminal discreditation of the
facts of her appearance.[16] Words like "seemingly," "allegedly," and "contradictory" began seeping out about this
child. Others who spoke for her—her mother, her lawyers,
her counselors—were subjected to an abusive media trial of
their credibility. But Tawana Brawley never spoke on the
record of her kidnapping, perhaps, and understandably, fur-

ther and more deeply traumatized into silence by the spectacle of what was happening around her. Speaking out is a dangerously engaged practice for black women.

There is no necessary consonance in these evocative moments. Although the relative calm of prejudice is interrupted, breaking our silence about our bodies does not always salve the wounds that racism and sexism inflict. In Toni Morrison's *The Bluest Eye*, Pecola has no success fighting the fracture of racism and abuse.[17] Her effort to escape her parents' horrific battles are directed toward invisibility and fracture, not away from it. "Please, God,' she whispered. . . . 'Please make me disappear.'. . . Little parts of her body faded away. . . . Her fingers . . . her arms . . . her feet. . . . The face was hard. . . . Only her tight, tight eyes were left. They were always left" (39). Pecola sat "long hours . . . looking in the mirror, trying to discover the secret of the ugliness.' (39). We might easily bring Lacan's notion of fragilization as an aspect of the schizoid into a critical perspective as we gaze at Pecola's gaze. Fracture and invisibility were her inheritance, but an empowering evocation does not overcome her silence. Pecola has no strength to "turn anything out" but her own wounded soul. Deprived of spiritual solace, Pecola is forced into a muddled and mad silence where no one ever speaks to her and where her victimization continues, unchecked. Pecola Breedlove is Tawana Brawley's literary sister.

In contrast to the failed voices of Tawana and Pecola, Alice Walker's Celie, who has been warned never to tell, does reap benefit from her mirrored gaze and her articulation of its vision. When Celie looks at her "naked self in the looking glass," the powerfully etched contrasts of her black and female body confront her gaze. "My hair is short and kinky. . . . My skin dark. My nose just a nose. My lips just lips. My body just any woman's body going through the changes of age." Celie's voice encourages and accompanies her specular moment. The narrative continues, "I talk to myself a lot, standing in front of the mirror" (220). An earlier scene of Celie's mirrored empowerment occurs at Shug's initiation and illustrates how our female bodies, these publicly negotiated sites of exchange, confrontation, and positionality, are available for our own private control.

> Here, take this mirror and go look at yourself down there. . . . I stand there with the mirror. . . . I lie back on the bed and haul up my dress. Yank down my bloomers. Stick the looking glass tween my legs . . . my pussy lips be black . . . inside look like a wet rose . . . I haul up my dress and look at my titties . . . I touch it with my finger. A little shiver go through me. . . . just enough to tell me this the right button to mash. (69,70)

As she experiments with masturbation for the first time, this sensual moment causes Celie her first experience with sexual pleasure.[18] The shiver tells Celie that she has found the right spot. Her words have empowering substance. Celie is so generously disposed toward Shug for encouraging this discovery of her sensuality, that she gives Shug (her husband's mistress) permission to sleep with Mr.————. "I don't care if you sleep with him, I say." Shug "take me at my word. I take me at my word too" (70). Her word and her body become her own, and the masturbatory release from fingering her "little button" and stroking her "titties" gives her sexual pleasure. There is an implicit contractual exchange here. The commodity of her body's sensuality, misused as it has been by her husband and father, becomes the exchangeable item. But this time, Celie initiates, controls, and executes the contract. She claims intimate ownership of her own self—both her body, and her psyche. And the pleasure she has learned to extract from her body is paired with the empowerment of her words.

I want to underscore that the trajectory from our physical bodies to our spiritual selves is neither consistent nor linear. The argument I make in *Moorings and Metaphors*—that fracture and shift articulate the spiraling narratives of black women's literatures—is true here as well.[19] The conflict I note here—the mirrored reflection of a prejudicial gaze versus a reflexive, self-mediated vision of our bodies—is ofttimes centered in language. However, when image and voice are severed, we lose an essential and life-affirming mediation.

In American culture, and in the imaginative representations of that culture in literature, our compromised environments often allow publicly constructed racial and sexual identities to supersede private consciousness. The result may be a negative dialectic—an "enabled" activity (or language) that dangerously rehearses the dynamics of racism and sexism. We saw this dialectic in practice when Anita Hill faced the fourteen senators of the Judiciary Committee. With little difficulty, we suspect this discourse was also a factor during the Wheatley hearings in 1771. Angela Davis reminds us of the pervasiveness of abuse directed toward women in American history:

> Throughout Afro-American women's economic history sexual abuse has been perceived as an occupational hazard. In slavery, Black women's bodies were considered to be accessible at all times to the slavemaster. In "freedom" there is ample documentation that as maids and washerwomen, Black women have been repeatedly the victims of sexual assault.[20]

As I read Davis's recitation of abuse, I think again about the motivation of Phillis Wheatley's slavemaster. He championed her cause, even to the extent of participating in the negotiations of her examination. Why would this white colonial landowner come to the passioned defense of his seventeen-year-old house slave? Davis suggests that we remember the direct relationship of sexual violence "as it is mediated by racial, class, and governmental violence and power" (47). The positions of Wheatley and Hill—enslaved and employed by legislated powerhouses, and then surrounded in *oral* (I do intend this double entendre) examination by a gathered body politic—gain a disturbing dimension.

The stories that script themselves into our contemporary politics form an impressive intersection. Anita and Phillis; Hagar, Celie, and Willa Nedeed; Desiree, Robin, and Tawana; and Patricia Williams, my grandmother, and Lorene Cary subvert and challenge the cultural biotext of legislative racism. These women, both fictive and compellingly real, insist themselves into the subject position of cultural theories of blackwomen's identities. Essential and actual images within our public and private cultures oblige our attention to women whose bodies contextualize our responses. Recall that in 1993, University of Pennsylvania Law Professor Lani Guinier was not even allowed to speak before the Senate Judiciary Committee in defense of her troubled nomination to a post in the Justice Department. Not to be similarly silenced, and rather than run the risk of losing control over their image-making mechanisms, the media fixed us on her body (especially her hair). The mean-spirited visual caricatures (especially a *New Republic* drawing) were accompanied by another oft-repeated sneering caricature of her "strange name, strange hair, strange ideas."[21] The media manipulated her words out of the contexts she had created for them in her legal writing. Guinier's legal writing (all we had as evidence of her speech) was so fractured and her image so caricatured—with her hair

Professor Lani Guinier addresses students at Duke Law School a few months after President Bill Clinton withdrew Guinier's nomination for the post of the U.S. assistant attorney general for civil rights. Duke University photo by Les Todd

as the identifying mark—that rescuing the two (language and body) would be an effort so futile that even her appearance on Ted Koppel's *Nightline* could not assist.

The metaphor of the mirrored body—facing its blackness and femaleness with the same sight as it is faced by others—gains dimensionality when it reneges on the contractual silence of its politicized position. The code of silence is broken once it gives voice and language to its story from the discrete positionality that cultural and gender politics have enforced within the dimensions of our literary and cultural histories. As the contemporary literature of African American writers provocatively indicates, and as the historical and contemporary experiences of African American women have consistently documented, giving our bodies our voices is a troubled enterprise.

My Tongue Is in My Friend's Mouth

In 1987, when I wrote the introduction to my study of Zora Neale Hurston, I recalled the process of my writing as including a constant stream of explanations and conversations with friends, family, neighbors, and colleagues as to who Hurston was and why I was writing about her. I concluded in that introductory gloss to *The Character of the Word* that I would probably always, in some form, still be writing about Zora.[22]

I had no idea then how right my notion would be. Even though Anita Hill and Phillis Wheatley are women whose experiences are divided by two centuries, Zora Hurston is kin to them. Hurston's own courtroom experience has eerie parallels to Hill's and Wheatley's. Accused in the late 1940s of a morals offense against two juvenile boys, Hurston found herself hysterical and prostrate on a courtroom floor in New York City, desperately trying to defend herself against these allegations. The fact that she had just completed a novel (*Seraph on the Suwanee*) in which a character had searched for a "knowing and a doing kind of love" was entered into the courtroom record as if it were verification of the charges against her.[23] Her words, a fiction, became a fact of her testimony. Like Anita Hill, Hurston's experience became front-page news—and in African American communities especially, their stories resonated with an uncomfortable familiarity. The public space of their citizenship was occupied territory—a nationally imposed border of racialized violence and sexualized abuse and stereotype.

Ironically, Hurston, who wrote in her autobiography that she had mystical visions of significant events in her life while still a child, may have anticipated that courtroom scene.[24] In her 1937 novel, *Their Eyes Were Watching God*, her character Janie has to face a trial by a white jury after she shoots her lover Tea Cake. Although the jury decides that Janie's actions were legitimate and necessary self-defense, the black community castigates her and maliciously criticizes her behavior: "They were all against her, she could see. So many were there against her that a light slap from each one of them would have beat her to death. She felt them pelting her with dirty thoughts. They were there with their tongues cocked and loaded" (275). Much of their criticism is directed toward her appearance, as if it justified their antipathy: "Aw, you know dem white mens wuzn't gointuh do nothin' tuh no woman dat look lak her" (280). Nonetheless the weight of her testimony does not move the hearts of the critical crowd. Even when Janie leaves the community she has shared with

Tea Cake and returns home, her appearance continues to cause spiteful commentary:

> "What she doin' coming back here in dem overhalls? Can't she find no dress to put on? . . . What dat ole forty year ole 'oman doin' wid her hair swingin' down her back lak some young gal?" . . . The porch couldn't talk for looking. The men noticed her firm buttocks like she had grape fruits in her hip pockets; the great rope of black hair swinging to her waist and unraveling in the wind like a plume; then her pugnacious breasts trying to bore holes in her shirt. They, the men, were saving with the mind what they lost with the eye. The women took the faded shirt and muddy overalls and laid them away for remembrance. It was a weapon against her strength. (10, 11)

My father recalls the passioned response in the African American community when Hurston's courthouse experience made two-inch-high headlines in the Baltimore *Afro-American* newspaper. Barber shops, fraternity and sorority meetings, and club meetings all rehearsed the details of the news stories—pelting her with their own dirty thoughts. All indications point to the fact that Hurston "turned it out." She used a Clarence Thomas–like defense. bell hooks writes that Clarence Thomas

> clearly strategized. . . . [He] dropped the mask of rational cool and expressed anger and rage at the process. His declaration that he was a victim of a "high-tech lynching" was a shrewd move which not only deflected away from the victimization of Anita Hill; it shifted the nature of the public discourse. Prior to these comments, race had not been seen as a primary factor shap-

ing the contents of the interrogations. By raising the historical specter of lynching, Thomas evoked images that are both racial and sexual in nature.[25]

Hurston seemed similarly astute. She claimed that her arrest "smacks of an anti-Negro violation of one's civil rights . . . [and if] such injustice can happen to one who has prestige and contacts, then there can be absolutely no justice for the little people of this community."[26] Hurston had already been a critical lightning rod in the community. Her associations with Harlem artists and New York patrons had earned her the antipathy of not a few of the black intelligentsia and rising middle class who felt that her racialized ethics that celebrated the separate culture of black folk challenged their goal of a quiet integration into America's culture of whiteness. Hurston's sexuality was also an unresolved item of gossip. *The Afro-American*'s story about her arrest quoted a reviewer's comments about her latest novel in which "Miss Hurston revealed intimate physical details about her central character 'to the point of absurdity,' but said the author had to 'construct a visible Freudian fretwork to give us understanding of herself.' "[27]

As late as 1985, one of the patriarchs of African American literary criticism, who was senior enough to have known Hurston, began a conference session dedicated to a critical discussion of Hurston as an author with an announcement that "Zora was a woman of many *strange* tastes." He drew out his pronunciation of "strange," lingering over the tone he knew it would suggest. Even though his comment was met with stinging rebuke from the audience, this intimation of his privately held opinion had already made its public impact. His comment put her on trial all over again as the conference session quickly lost its academic austerity and

Novelist, anthropologist, and folklorist Zora Neale Hurston photographed in 1934 by Carl Van Vechten. Yale Collection of American Literature, Beinecke Rare Book & Manuscript Library, Yale University

shifted into a passionate call and response between the distinguished panelists and the audience of (generally younger) scholars.[28]

Public admonitions of black women's conduct too often dissolve into public displays of their bodies. Many of these moments share enough of the scripted violence that citizenship (or slavery) has imposed on black women until their shared text is something black women like me find too intimate and familiar. In a contemporary discourse that seems to engage crisis encounters like those experienced by the women I have noted as crises of psychological and/or spiritual identity, the essential, shared feature in this struggle is actually quite superficial—it is the body, not the self.

Hill gained painful perspective on an embodied reality like the one the hearings displayed. Her post-hearings posture and thoughtful, often literary, reflectiveness in those public forums even compared her own experience to Hurston's. From the stoic finesse of her televised testimony, Hill moved to another stage in the public arena and indicated a reflective thoughtfulness that the hearings did not reveal. She had experienced a moment of facing, an event that made it clear to her that regardless of her stature within a professional community, her identity as a professor of law, and the days and nights of education and classical training that this identity entails, there comes some essentialist moment when she must acknowledge that one of the elements to vie for control of her public life is purely physical.

Actually, the mirror captures not only the image, but the sustained glare of those who sit on the other side of the inquisitory bench. I do not care what questions they are asking, or what century it is, or what text they use as a basis for interrogation—poetry, the intersections of literary language and real life passion, or sworn affidavits and depositions—the inquisition sustains its force because the body on the other side is dark and female.

I think the intimacy between Hill's moment, Hurston's encounter, and Hagar's (*Song of Solomon*) realization is somewhat like French feminist philosopher Luce Irigaray's sense of "nearness," which she describes in *This Sex Which Is Not One* as a "ceaseless exchange of herself with the [O]ther." Especially as Irigaray identifies nearness as a "defense of desire through speech," her imagery lends a critical depth to the shared intimacies that our voiced narratives seem to recover.[29]

When Alice Walker published *The Color Purple* in 1977, the riveting public dialogue focused on her characters Celie and Shug and argued long and loudly about whether or not Walker should or should not have allowed the public spaces of her novel to reveal the dynamics of their intimate relationship. I know we also talked and wrote about all the other dimensions of this story, but in my kitchen, with my mother and sisters, it was Celie and Shug we talked about. Mr._____ was an Invisible Man.

In my classes, the lesbian relationship in this novel provokes the most vehement criticism. Much of this criticism comes from African American women students who mightily resist the self-saving love that Celie and Shug's physical intimacy recovers. I was very surprised that the reaction in my mother's kitchen was not very different from the one in my classrooms. Although I am not certain that my mother and younger sister would today have the same argument that we had in 1977—that Walker told too much, that she made it up, that it was not credible—then, they felt absolutely sure that Walker had crossed the lines of propriety.

bell hooks recognizes the power of this novel's public identity, noting that works like *The Color Purple* "captivate readers not by covert reference to sexual matters but by explicit exposure and revelation."[30] Celie's letters to God and her sister (her way of circumventing the warning not to tell) contain the details of sexuality in graphic style, where Celie is "not only the speaking sex, the desiring sex; she is talking sex." hooks suggests that the letters serve as a "screen . . . keep[ing] the reader at a distance, creating the illusion of intimacy where there is none."[31] Our public cultures would like to make an illusory intimacy out of what hooks labels "illusion[s] of intimacy." When Walker brings us near (in the sense of Irigaray's "nearness") the emotional passion that the relationship between Celie and Shug enables, the intimacy also engages the voyeuristic and damaging "nearness" that characterizes the dis/ease with lesbianism in African American communities.

The public's discomfort with sexuality between and among women within African American literatures reflects the discomfort of our public cultures with sexuality and passion that resist patriarchy and its power as it is instead enabled, sustained, and shared (in this instance) between women. After all, the bias of heterosexuality promises one of the few spheres of privilege in our culture that is equally available to whites and blacks. It is as if the "normative" promise of heterosexuality's masculinist authority promises to extend this norm and its authority to our communities whose ethnicity has historically devalued and challenged any expressive power. So, the abusive and conservative sexual ethics of homophobia are generated in some significant measure from the veneer of power that heterosexuality has successfully asserted in black and white communities. Public denigration of queerness perversely uplifts a publicly denigrated ethnicity.

In the 1960s, African American college students like me were deprived of poet Audre Lorde's mentorship and teaching when administrative officials at historically black colleges allowed their homophobia to halt her visiting (poet-in-) residency. I was a student at Talladega College in Alabama. We had a virtual parade of black artists who stopped to visit our classrooms, galleries, and chapel pulpit, sharing their artistry with us. The administration may have later regretted a visit by Stokely Carmichael (now Kwame Toure), but his radicalism did not ban him from our campus as did Lorde's sexuality. I remember poets Julia Fields and (then) Don Lee reading their newest works in my English classes. Lee (now Haki Madhubuti) would always come with boxloads of his latest chapbooks to sell. Soprano Carol Brice and pianist Thomas Flagg were among those who headlined our concert artist series and Robert Earl Jones dramatically rendered both Shakespeare and Dunbar in public readings. I do not recall how I learned that Audre Lorde, who was visiting at Tougaloo College (in Mississippi), was pulled off the tour. And I do not know the circumstances of the termination. I was well aware, however, that one of the poets on that circuit was "discovered" to be lesbian, and that that discovery was enough to halt her participation in what had become the customary exchange of these scholars and artists across our UNCF (United Negro College Fund) campuses. What an unhappy irony that censorship occasioned as it initiated my political education into the despairing connections of racism and sexism. It helped me learn to respect the breadth, reach, and intimacy of ignorance and prejudice.

Throughout the twentieth century, within black women's literatures and within our communities, my teenaged loss of Audre Lorde's graceful presence is consistently and substantively replicated. The ways are not similar. But the passionate response and the spiritual loss that follow sexism and racism are too often the same. The contemporary feature of this debate has considerable relevance to the historical politics that black and female bodies impose on issues like sexuality and women's rights. Before these discussions erupted in the public arenas of talk shows or feminist criticisms of literatures, the public discomfort with lesbianism (specifically lesbianism in black women's literature) was already being acknowledged by some novels of the 1920s and 1930s that hinted at the intimacies characteristic of the sexual and spiritual dimensions of lesbianism, but did not dare pass the realm of intimation.[32] Perhaps in anticipation of the public's homophobia, the acknowledgment was a closeted disclosure—an intimated subtext in a literature that was publicly received as centered in a heterosexual discourse. This literature could only hint at the intimacies characteristic of the sexual dimensions of lesbianism. The public's approbation (which would be an economic as well as a social issue for those who published) did not allow this subtext to venture past the realm of intimation. One point seems to remain constant in historic literary and contemporary public cultures. The damage done by public intimations of sexual intimacies between women parallels the violent and abusive subtexts that follow literary intimacies between black women.

It is ironic and telling that the public and disorderly conduct that followed the publication of *The Color Purple* was due in great measure to the presumably abridged divide between private and public. The nonsense that characterized much of the debate is probably best represented in recalling journalist Tony Brown's declaration on a Phil Donahue show that was taped in the midst of the public outcry about the Walker novel. Brown argued that, despite the fact that *he had not read the book*, he was absolutely certain that no lesbian relationship could take the place of love between a black man and a black woman. One wonders what judgment could have been rendered had he made the radical move to "read the subject" (a.k.a. "the book").

In a disconcertingly parallel fashion, one of the many conversations about filmmaker Julie Dash's film *Daughters of the Dust* concerned the lesbian relationship between her characters Yellow Mary and Trula.[33] In this film that reconstructs a Gullah family reunion on a South Carolina island, one of the Peazant women (Eula) admonishes a group of aunts, cousins, and sisters who shun their kinship to Mary. Eula says "If you love yourselves, then love Yellow Mary, because she's a part of you. Just like we're a part of our mothers. A lot of us are going through things we feel we can't handle all alone." In an uncomfortable reminder of the way that art replicates life, Dash revealed, in a discussion with bell hooks, that the intense publicity garnered by this film led the actress who played Yellow Mary to argue in public forums (interviews and guest appearances) that she was never supposed to be gay in the film. However, Dash tells hooks unequivocally that Yellow Mary and Trula were "very clearly lovers."[34]

In Gloria Naylor's novel *The Women of Brewster Place*, Mattie's reflection is similar to Dash's Yellow Mary.[35] The community's discovery that its two new neighbors are lesbian leads to their derision and alarm about their "difference." But Mattie Michael, a matriarchal-type figure who reminds her neighbors and friends that she has "loved women too . . . some women deeper than I ever loved any man," defends this desire, speaks out, and echoes Eula Peazant's admonition. Mattie suggests that "Maybe it's not so different. Maybe that's why some women get so riled up . . . 'cause they know deep down it's not so different after all" (141).

Irigaray (whose phrasing is recalled in "defend[ing] desire") inscribes both Mattie's and Eula's sense of closeness and intimacy with one's self in her figure of two lips, which "keep women in touch with her self, without distinguishing what is touching from what is being touched." Irigaray's compelling imagery specifies a place for touch. In contrast, Zora Neale Hurston's character Janie (*Their Eyes Were Watching God*) specifies a space for voice.[36] I am drawn to the parallel visions of nearness and intimacy, and speech and voice that Janie's declaration draws together.

In *Their Eyes Were Watching God*, Janie encourages her friend Phoeby to tell her story for her. Since she returned to her home in Eatonville after Tea Cake's death and the humiliating moments of her public trial, the neighbors' eager anticipation to learn what happened to Janie has been the riveting subject of porch gossip. After Janie relates her story to Phoeby, she instructs her best friend to carry this narrative to the neighborhood. She trusts Phoeby with this message, claiming their nearness with a signifying intimacy: "mah tongue is in mah friend's mouf" (17). The narrative voice explains that Janie and her friend Phoeby had been "kissin friends" and suggests that it is this already established intimacy that allows Janie to gift Phoeby with the closest touch of all—her story. There is an inescapable sexual subtext within this exchange.

The environment of Janie's and Phoeby's meeting supports and encourages the intimations of intimacy. It is "dusk-dark"—a moment in the Eatonville community where night has not yet descended but when daylight is waning. Phoeby comes into Janie's yard by "the intimate gate" and they sit alone in the lengthening shadows on the porch. Although Phoeby eventually leaves Janie, she does not do so until she is fully satisfied (satiated?) with the intimacy and passion of their exchange (a.k.a. Janie's story). Janie's physical and spiritual "nearness" to her friend allows Phoeby to figuratively carry (embody) her text. Janie shares a poetic principle with

Phoeby and the evocation, the telling, of her story dissolves what is traditionally understood as a divide between the private and public. Her willingness to share voice and text and to encourage Phoeby to carry this story to their neighbors recasts their private intimacy into a public act. Their exchange illustrates how sexuality, imagination, intimacy, and intimation can occupy a shared space between public enactments and private encounters.

Intimate acts work their way through socially constructed grammars, whose codes of public conduct encourage them to emerge finally as veiled and unrecognizable events. If we cast aside the kind of hesitation that characterized Tony Brown's response to Walker's novel, the HBCU's reaction to Audre Lorde's sexuality, and even the silencing discord in my mother's kitchen, we could speculate in a rewarding way on the relationship between homosexual ideologies and literary uses of voice, language, creativity, and generation. Within such speculation, the presumed intimacy of the speaking black voice can be positioned next to an intimate creativity. It is as if the potential Phoeby engages to reflect Janie's story is, metaphorically, merely one step away from a potential to be otherwise engaged with Janie.

When Toni Morrison reflected on the Hill/Thomas hearings, she reminded us of the dangers in public hearings, noting that "broken silence" and "disobedient speech" both find in themselves an association with bondage and victimization.[37] In American culture, and in the imaginative representations of that culture in literature, our compromised environments valorize publicly constructed racial and sexual identities, but they do not support privately authored identities that may be at odds with public representations.

The perverse consequence of public discussion is that the public realm has become a brutal and reductive battleground for sexual politics. Violence associated with recent legislative initiatives to protect and/or articulate the rights of gays and lesbians testifies to this. Angela Davis recalls June Jordan's "Poem About My Rights" in her discussion about the relationships between sexuality, violence, and power.[38] Jordan's poem laments her inability to walk safely and with self-assurance through her neighborhood without making radical changes to her clothing, her carriage, "gender-identity," her age, and her "status as a woman." Jordan concludes that her lament is prompted because of her inability to control her own body "because I am the wrong / sex the wrong age the wrong skin."[39]

Davis uses the imagery of this poem to explain her point that "to comprehend the nature of sexual violence . . . we must be cognizant of its social mediations."[40] The courthouse scene in *Their Eyes Were Watching God*, Hurston's own courtroom experience, and the parallels of both of these to the event of Anita Hill's 1991 testimony and Phillis Wheatley's 1772 episode illustrate the ways in which physical and spiritual violence are intimate partners whenever the black woman's body metonymically displays her mouth and implicates her voice.

Hurston never recovered from the trauma of her experience in the New York courtroom. In *The Character of the Word*, I suggest that Hurston's subsequent retreat from New York's artistic scene was due in great measure to her loss of control over what had been a carefully constructed public identity. I continue to believe in the accuracy of that observation. Contemporary events that publicly exhibit the black woman's body—in literature, film, academic conferences, or Senate chambers—are evidence that black women's bodies are a conflicted site. No wonder Hurston's final paragraph in her autobiography's chapter on love reads so ambivalently.

> But pay no attention to what I say about love. . . .
> Anybody whose mouth is cut cross-ways is given to
> lying, unconsciously as well as knowingly. So pay my
> few scattering remarks no mind as to love in general. I
> know only my part.[41]

Although this insistent articulation does replace the abusive
silence that has yoked black women's voices, the irony is that
we are also compromised by the public spaces of their enact-
ment. Consider the following heartbreaking event as evidence
of the depth of this loss.

In the nineteenth century, Victorian prudery did not
subvert the public and nude display of two African women,
both renamed "Sara Bartmann" in Great Britain and France.
Her given name was not as important as the "icon" of black
sexuality she came to represent. Sander Gilman, a professor of
the history of psychiatry, has researched the history of this
event, drawing attention to an essay in the 1819 *Dictionary of
Medical Sciences* that summarized contemporary "views on the
sexual nature of black females." J. J. Virey's essay noted their
" 'voluptuousness' is 'developed to a degree of lascivity unknown in our climate for their sexual organs are much more
developed than those of whites.' "[42]

Nineteenth-century perspectives on black women's
bodies telescoped and exploited this pornographic curiosity.
Our bodies were "widely perceived as possessing not only a
'primitive' sexual appetite but also the external signs of this
temperament—'primitive' genitalia." Eighteenth-century ex-
peditions to Africa gratified Europeans' perverted curiosities,
assuring them an objective focus. An 1810 exhibition in Lon-
don featured "Saartjie Baartman, also called Sarah Bartmann or
Saat-Jee and known as the 'Hottentot Venus.' " She was not the
sole victim of this kind of exploitation. In 1829 another

woman of Africa, also called " 'the Hottentot Venus' . . . was the prize attraction at a ball given by the Duchess Du Barry in Paris." _____ died in France after five years of displayed, exhibitory abuse.[43] Her name, left behind in her homeland, was not important to preserve. Her body displaced her identity which was consumed by the conduct of a culture's abusive ethics. _____ was merely twenty-five years old when she died. Gilman's judgment, that "the figure of Sarah Bartmann was reduced to her sexual parts," is not metaphor. Her body was dissected and her "genitalia and buttocks" were forensically preserved and made available to both medical and lay audiences for their sustained consideration.

The San/Koi (Khoisan) females, black women of South Africa who were first victimized by the Dutch in the seventeenth century, contained enough exoticism to make their bodies the prize of European anthropological inquiry—the "other" enterprise of colonialism. The thesis of Gilman's scholarly discussion is to compare her to white prostitutes of the era, whose industry is also enabled by white male patriarchy and who are also the victims of a disfiguring gaze—a passion of sexual rather than scholarly dominance. But the comparative assessment lacks balance. The disfigurement repeated by the black woman's death and dissection seem to carry the weight of the abuse. Particularly disturbing to me is the fact that Gilman's generously illustrated scholarly text repeats the Victorian exhibit, in a manner discomfitingly parallel to its voyeuristic thesis. Both the original exhibit and the exhibitory text are driven by the "riveting" anomaly of the black woman's "organ[s] of generation."

There are no records of the words of either woman. And the dissected remains have been absorbed into the records of Europe's imperialist history. Gilman's scholarly essay does remain. But in addition to its scholarship, it is a repetitive gesture of the first colonizing act. It clarifies the way in which the black woman's reduction to one synedochic posture of her sexuality reveals the dangers in giving voice and language to our story from the discrete positionality that sexual identity enforces on our literary and cultural histories. Whoever tells this story, the victims or the voyeurs, risks this danger. So although the dimension of voice remains a troubled region in the literature of African American women, it is clear that provocative and courageous imaginations negotiate this space. Black women who live and tell the fictive legacy of America's cultural politics insist on their right to place their tongues anywhere they choose.

The Long Way Home

First, we got a box of heavy flow, night-wear, super absorbency Kotex. This was before the days when the Kimberly-Clark folk filled super thin sanitary napkins with some kind of super absorbent crystals. When I was in junior high, absorbency of the kind we required meant an incredibly thick pad. After all, we needed to block all the water in the swimming pool at Fillmore Junior High School. Then, we stuffed these pads into a stocking with a run in it. This was before the age of panty hose too. After we had a stocking filled with enough Kotex to circle our heads, we put these into a plastic bag and wrapped it around our precious pressed hair. Only then would we leave the girls' locker room and enter the swimming pool area. Our only source of comfort was that it was seventh period.

We learned to be aggressive and assertive about class schedules in junior high. Black girls just had to have a seventh period, end-of-the-day physical education class. We'd even give up the elite chorus group, a late-day study hall, orchestra, and yearbook staff—all of which met during seventh period—the semester we were scheduled to swim. Priorities, you know. If all our trappings failed, we could leave school immediately after swimming and make certain that no one would see us because we could go home the long way.

It was one of the few times I was grateful for my older sister's presence in my school. Who else could have taught me how to stuff the Kotex into my swimming cap with as much consideration as she extended to me? After all, Karen didn't want my nappy-headed self embarrassing her on her way home. So it was mutually beneficial that she should wrap my head as thoroughly as she could. Our huddle in the corner of the locker room, checking each other's Kotex, stuffing escaped plastic back under our caps, making certain there were no gaps in the loop around our heads kept us there until Miss Zimmerman's very last whistle, when she insisted we close the locker-room doors and enter the swimming pool area.

The only time I really remember my preparations being a total failure was the time I was forced off the diving board. They thought I was sinking when I failed to come back to the surface and strike out for the side of the pool. But that wasn't it at all. It was the whoosh of water I felt when I jumped in that went right past my Kotex covered ears and started seeping through my scalp that paralyzed me. I could feel every strand of my hair react to the watery assault. Cold watery streams viciously attacked my roots, oblivious to the intensity of my locker-room efforts. I was so distressed over what I knew was going on under my cap that I forgot to stroke out from the jump. I just sank. It was when I felt the poke of the nine-foot metal pole that Miss Zimmerman kept for just such an emergency (drowning bodies, not drenched hair) that I remembered to grab hold. They dragged me to the side of the pool and she tapped me on my rubberized head as she always did when she wanted our attention. I think she knew the black girls had an extra hard time hearing with all that cotton, plastic, and nylon stocking-net around our ears. "What happened?" she asked. I shook my head. "Do you want to try it again?" I quickly climbed out, said no, and hurried for the locker room. The buzzer had rung anyway. I do not even remember how my hair looked after I removed the sopping mass from around my head. It is one of those repressed, childhood memories. Where was the age of baseball caps when you needed it? I do remember, however, that I took the long way home.

African American women have learned well how and when to hide our bodies. Sometimes a lesson in public assault was an instructive moment. But at other times, the history of racist and sexist aesthetics has made us hate our hair and mask our bodies, and has encouraged the desperation of Kotex on our heads—or sedate teal blue dresses. At what cost this dissembling? When we mask in these ways, we actually, and perversely, privilege the gaze of others. The bodies that emerge when others control our images are disfigured and fragmented. Consider, for example, the annoying verbiage of television's sportscasters who were supposed to comment on the skating of Olympic figure skaters Deborah Thomas and Surya Bonaly (from France), but who could not tear themselves away from what their bodies did *not* represent in skating iconography. Other (white) skaters were graceful. These two dark and elegant skaters were athletic. Other (white) skaters were artistic, except Tonya Harding, whose "blackening" by the unappreciative media included emphasizing her athleticism. Thomas and Bonaly were technical. One National Public Radio discussion on Bonaly's costume during

Comedian Whoopi Goldberg and others appear on Donahue *to promote* "Comic Relief '90." *AP/Wide World Photos*

the Winter 1994 Olympics bewailed her choice of pastel colors, worrying that they would unfortunately heighten the contrast of her dark skin. Neither skater could shatter the fair-skinned icon of the ideal figure skater.

Similarly riveted to a black body was entertainment culture's gossipy and startled reaction to Whoopi Goldberg's short-lived relationship with actor Ted Danson. They were certainly not Hollywood's first interracial couple. Neither was Goldberg the first to occasion a marriage's rupture (Danson left his wife to pursue the relationship with Goldberg). However, because Goldberg's dark body had resisted the whitening gaze through which Hollywood had "integrated" other black actresses into its ranks, the pairing between this "Hollywood Hunk" and Goldberg made terrific press. Her dreadlocks,

Jewish surname and provocative first name, darkened lips, racialized discourse, and lived-stereotype past (she had, at one time, supported her infant daughter on welfare) fractured the images Hollywood seems to encourage for black women actors. Her film history itself speaks to the visual and textual conundrum her body represents. There is a dramatic and provocative difference between the Goldberg who played Celie in Steven Spielberg's version of *The Color Purple* and the Goldberg of films like *Sister Act*, *Ghost*, and especially *Made in America*. The latter film, heralded as the first on-screen romance for Goldberg, cast Danson as her love interest. The encounters between them, hardly love scenes of the traditional variety, were instead classic Hollywood comedic buffoonery. They were dramatically different from what her viewing audience had been led to expect by the advertisements that promised a romantic encounter between Goldberg and Danson. We had not anticipated the encounter would be painful-to-watch slapstick. Perhaps however, the inept fumbling between Danson and Goldberg as they fell over furniture, yelled, hollered, and ineffectually groped at each other, was exactly what one should have expected from a woman whose body contradicted and resisted "classic" Hollywood images. When this film relationship left the screen and entered the tabloids, it carried along with it its resistant absurdity.

The media's review, marked by incredulous and puzzled commentary, of her relationship with Danson had not even reached its peak when he appeared at a Friar's Club roast for her, plastered in blackface makeup with a script that used as its comedic core her dark body and its sexual appetite for him. This moment of racist and sexist humormongering collected every stereotype and issue—visual, verbal, subliminal, straightforward, direct and indirect. It vivified the historical abuse that the embodied politics of blackness and femaleness involve in the United States. The fragmented and frenzied attack and defense the occasion enjoined characterizes the conflicted racial and sexual politics of our public cultures. Goldberg defended her lover—he abused her with her permission, she argued. She had even encouraged the blackface makeup. Eventually their relationship dissolved and he returned home to, at least temporarily, his (white) wife. The publicity garnered by their relationship, he would somewhat ironically comment, had become too challenging to the privacy they needed if it were to succeed.

The Friday Night Women were divided. She was literally *self*-destructive, some of us argued. It began with the name she chose over "Karen Johnson," her birthname. She was a victim of racism, or a victim of Danson, or a victim of herself, others of us asserted. We did agree that she had encouraged, facilitated, and promoted the use of her black body as a comedic target. Goldberg's pathetic public moment joins her to the ranks of women like Hill, Hurston, Hagar, Wheatley, and Willa who are startled into recognition that the bodily gaze comes both from within and without. Our power for change and self-definition only happens if we acknowledge the sight of others and control for that gaze. Goldberg's passionate self-embrace may have been weakened when she shared it with Danson. It was certainly disabled when others spoke more loudly and more assertively against her than she was able to speak for herself. B(l)ack talk has to be a consistent and passionate articulation.

If we lose our boldness and our passion, if we retreat away from the public response to black women's bodies—the historical stereotypes and the persistently racist and sexist dialogues they endure—we turn over to others who have no right to our privacy the very identities we believe our silence protects. bell hooks argues that passion can disrupt boundaries, articulating, in this deconstruction, a space where our differences encourage intimacy, nearness, and finally, redemption.

Redemption is critical not only for the injured, fragilized psyches of African American women who have relinquished boldness and passion, but for those whose bodies are different from ours. They allow that identity patriarchal, racialist, or sexualized subordination of others. They lose their own souls, however, in the processes of patriarchy, racism, and sexism. So bound up are they in maintaining positions of power and authority, and so common to them is controlling, silencing language (like Clarence Thomas's response to the judiciary committee: "This, gentlemen, is nothing but a high-tech lynching") that the withering away of their own spirits is barely noticeable—until it is too late. Redemption would reconstitute their souls as well, giving them such passion and respect for themselves that they could not abuse others without the painful loss of those gains.

I do understand well my grandmother's red reluctance. A few years ago I braided my hair in a moment of needing, remembering, and understanding my grandmother. Two thick rope-like braids embrace my head now, holding me all in, I sometimes think, but mostly just reminding me of Celia.

When my daughter was a child, I braided her hair on the front porch. In twilight hours or warm summer mornings I worked intricately braided patterns into Ayana's hair, trying to capture some of that precious childhood time when my sisters and I could not have been closer to our mother or grandmothers Celia and Marguerite than we were when they were braiding our hair. We sat propped between their strong legs, our shoulders leaning against their soft thighs, feeling touched and safe. Tenderheaded or not, those were times when our bodies and theirs, intimately intertwined and held by the web of their fingers and our hair, were sweetly cared for, and immeasurably valued.

I have taken the long way home, back to my grandmothers' porch and stoop, my mother's kitchen, and my own spiritual space. I have a loving respect for their caution, having gained courage and thoughtful reflection from its example. And I am well aware that my current passion for red could only have been nurtured through the sure touch of their careful love.

CHAPTER TWO

Language, Thought, and Culture

English isn't a good language to express emotions in.
       —Nikki Giovanni, "My House"

Ross Perot addresses a black audience as "you people," and
we go ballistic. Rappers call our women "bitches and
'hos," and we develop lockjaw.
       —William Raspberry

I knew that words, despite the old saying, never fail. And
my reading had given me words to spare. . . . Surely I had
enough words to cover a moment's discomfort. I had
enough for hours if need be.
       —Maya Angelou, *I Know Why the Caged Bird Sings*

If poetry, like rap, is disruptive performance or . . .
articulation of the melancholia of the people's
wounding . . . then poetry can be defined . . . like rap, as
an audible or sounding space of opposition.
       —Houston A. Baker, Jr., *Black Studies, Rap and the
       Academy*

Word work is sublime . . . it makes meaning. . . . We *do*
language. That may be the measure of our lives.
       —Toni Morrison, Lecture to the Swedish Academy
       upon the occasion of the award of the Nobel Prize
       for Literature

On the day that Bill Clinton was sworn in as the forty-second president of the United States, millions of Americans and countless thousands citizens of other nations had the opportunity to discover for themselves the powerful cultural presence within Maya Angelou's poetry. Angelou had been asked to write a poem for the event. From the moment the request was made public, the gathered energy and anticipation of what was sure to be a soul-stirring moment was powerfully felt by all who knew, or who were familiar with, the history of her dramatic and passionate word work. However, when Angelou's inaugural moment arrived, her poem, "On the Pulse of Morning," was merely delivered.

More than one home in black America anticipated a powerful rendering that day rather than the quiet and relatively still delivery that instead marked Angelou's internationally broadcast moment. Many who had looked forward to "the poem" with significant anticipation were surprised that Angelou's verse did not resonate with the performative cultural marks we had come to expect from her. And black Americans were not the only ones who noticed the absence and/or loss of Angelou's characteristic rendering.

When media called upon academic as well as lay reviewers to make a public comment on the poem, at least one nationally known poet admiringly noted that it "wasn't emoted," that it was "really spoken." Others alluded to the difference between Angelou's traditional practice and that day's example and reported that "only hints" of her talent were apparent, and that her poem was "intentionally speech-like."[1] This commentary acknowledges the cultural divide between the expectations of intimacy between language and culture within an African American community, and the appreciation and respect that a culturally anonymous language earns outside of our community.

For years, both national and international audiences have been graced with the dynamic and dramatic presentation of Angelou's rendered verse. In public performances and in media events, her expressive flair as her hands sweep through the air and the visual ballet of her long, slim fingers are matched only by the rise and swell of her resonant voice. Her poetry, speeches, and public presentations have come to be celebrated and recognized for the way in which they articulate an African American cultural code. Until that inaugural moment, Angelou's public linguistic artistry had been testament and example of orature—a *rendered* practice of artistic black language. But something masked Angelou's culture that day.

It may have been stuffed beneath the veil of political agenda that called for "change"—a Clintonian/new democratic version of America that foregrounded the struggles of class against class, and that would draw these battle lines at the cost of culture. The gathered anticipation of African Americans was something reminiscent of that old excitement of the 1960s, when phones jangled throughout neighborhoods, interrupting parties on the party line with the message "colored people on t.v.!" Maya Angelou's culture was contained in her color. Neither her voice, her demeanor, nor, some would argue, the text of her poem, collaborated in a performance that honored African American tradition. Those traditions have been practiced and refined throughout this century in African American families—those same genera-

Poet Maya Angelou recites "On the Pulse of Morning" during the 1993 presidential inauguration ceremonies. AP/Wide World Photos

tions who had gathered to hear Angelou's rendering of "On the Pulse of Morning."

It is interesting to note here, that when Janet Jackson plays the role of Justice in director John Singleton's "Afrocentric street romance," *Poetic Justice*, Jackson easily renders the script's verse—lines that Angelou herself has authored.[2] She emphasizes the performative power of Angelou's text, uncovering the cultural resonance of these words so that we feel their embrace of the dimensions of her character's life. When Singleton's movie was released in the summer of 1993, I thought again about the inaugural poem. The contrast between its quiet delivery and the cultural resonance that Jackson invested in her performance of Angelou's verse for the movie was dramatic. The comparison emphasized again Angelou's curious distancing of culture from the inaugural event.

Many African Americans had their first experience with rendering as an audience to or presenter of James Weldon Johnson's poetic sermon "The Creation," one of seven in Johnson's 1927 collection, *God's Trombones*.[3] In communities across this nation, some twentieth-century youngsters did not make their debuts in the heavily starched white shirts, organdy dresses, rustling crinolines, and vaseline-shined patent leather shoes—the official dress for Jack and Jill cotillions. Some girls did not first appear on their fathers' arms and with teenaged escorts (often commissioned and approved for that event only) at sorority-sponsored debutante balls, where, after the debate about twenty-button or fourteen-button gloves had been resolved, they made their well-practiced curtseys before the a.k.a. (also known as) scholarship pageant audiences. And for young men only "beautillions"—a late-century black elite (corrective) nod to the sexism of the debutante event—were not the traditional forums for these youngsters' first public introductions.[4] Instead, there are generations of youngsters whose entry into public community life occurred at the moment they stepped up to a podium and flung their voices out to a congregation of family and teachers and friends who awaited this moment of their children's inauguration into public adolescence.

I remember sitting transfixed in a church auditorium as some specially selected youngster matched his voice to the timbre of Johnson's words, rendering them as real as he possibly could: whispering when he spoke of the "cypress swamp" that was "darker than a hundred midnights"; pausing dramatically after declaring God's loneliness ("I'm lonely"); and slowly and carefully enunciating each word of His stunning solution to that dilemma ("I'll make me a world"). By the third repetition of God's assertion "That's good" (a compliment to the fine work of His creation), all the children in the auditorium, their parents, and I whispered along with the speaker, "That's good."

> And God stepped out onto space,
> And He looked around and said,
> "I'm lonely—I'll make me a world."
>
> And as far as the eye of God could see
> Darkness covered everything,
> Blacker than a hundred midnights
> Down in a cypress swamp.
> Then God smiled—and the light broke
> And the darkness rolled up on one side
> And the light stood shining on the other,
> And God said, "That's good."
>
> Then God reached out and took the light in His
>   hands

And God rolled the light around in His hands
Until He made the sun;
And He set that sun a-blazin in the heavens.
And the light that was left from making the sun
God gathered it up in a shining ball
And flung it against the darkness
Spangling the night with the moon and the stars.
Then down between the darkness and the light
He hurled the world;
And God said, "That's good."
                    —James Weldon Johnson, "The
                    Creation"

I remember as well my own first experience with "The Creation." My mother taught me to pause for two counts after each word in the author's name. As I spoke, the sound of the n in Weldon and Johnson buzzed and hung suspended in the hot, still air of the church basement. She told me to pause (for three counts) after I recited the poem's title—"The [*to rhyme with "me"*] Creation" [*one, two, three*]—and again after saying: "By James [*one, two*] Weldon [*one, two*] Johnson" [*one, two, three*]. Then I was directed to step up to the microphone in concert with the sermon's first line: "And God *stepped* out onto space."[5]

So when Angelou did not step or gesture, when she did not move at all around the small space of the inaugural platform, and especially, when she did not modulate or *culturate* her voice, African Americans like me felt quite keenly the loss of those cultural codes that could have marked that moment. Instead of the echoes of a celebratory rendering, we were left only with a printed text, which we needed to purchase and read after the event because she had given us no aural and no visual way to recall it. The flat, slim, but elegant editions of her poem appeared quickly next to cash registers in Waldenbooks and Barnes and Noble stores across the country, but we had none of the memories that have historically marked the formal events of African American language. Perhaps it was not the moment for culture.

After all, the Clinton administration's effort has been to make palatable the notion of a race-free public policy. The political quagmires of 1980s affirmative actions—an aggressive and assertive inscription of race into public policy—were too dangerous for a new administration, elected with much less than a public mandate, to negotiate. So the erasure of race as public policy may have been metaphorically reflected in Angelou's erasure of culture from her inaugural moment. But even that acknowledgment expresses a certain kind of loss.

Race Talk

Her name was Shahrazade. But one of the audience members of the *Donahue* show was so disgusted by what this woman was saying (the talk show talk that day was about black men) that the audience respondent said to her, "And you . . . whatever your name is, I can't even pronounce it . . ." and then proceeded to vehemently criticize whatever it was Shahrazade had said. Now wait a minute, I said. Shahrazade is too hard to say? "Anastasia" has more syllables. In my part of North Carolina, no one has trouble learning the pronunciation of the Duke University basketball coach (Kryzewski), so what's so hard about this name? I knew the name of this African American woman was not really the issue. It was her politics that were the issue. But we connect languages, names, characters, and politics so intimately in the United

States that our biases about one easily spill over from one category to the other.

Many times, we only need to look at a person to decide how our language prejudices will interact with them. One well-rehearsed (in academic circles) anecdote tells of an incident involving a network television station's report on the Ann Arbor, Michigan, court case where black parents were suing the school board because their children were being handicapped in the public schools.[6] The parents charged that teachers' negative attitudes and uninformed perspectives about their children's black dialects unnecessarily placed them into remedial classrooms, targeted them for special education, and made them consistently poor readers. When the network sent in a reporter and photographer to do a feature story on the school where the children's education was being contested, the nightly news program featured a reporter's voice-over as the camera panned a classroom, doing a close-up of a black child at her desk. The reporter's voice-over said something to the effect that these are the children whose language is unintelligible to their teachers. Nobody heard the child speak. It just happened that she was a youngster who used standard English both at home and at school, was an honor roll student, and whose parents were faculty members at the university. Her color, however, was enough to make the reporter and cameraperson assume that she was one of the speakers of nonstandard English and in enough academic difficulty that her parents were suing the district.

Public and educational policies have made a real mess out of language issues. At one point, well-intentioned educators felt that "dialect readers" were the way to teach nonstandard English–speaking children how to read. One series of readers produced for this effort was so filled with errors (in the dialect) that children in Chicago did not even recognize the language that was supposed to represent their "home talk." Inane and offensive programs intended to "bridge" students from their ethnic speech communities to the acultural standard English in textbooks were marketed based on the assumption that some children just could not learn to read as well as others because the dialects spoken in their homes were not like the dialects spoken in others. I always took great pleasure in pointing out to students in linguistics classes that no one ever suggested that a student whose nonstandard dialect in a U.S. classroom was British English (rather than Black English) needed a special reader to bridge them over to the standard. Yet the sound and vocabulary differences of British dialects are as nonstandard as those spoken by the population of speakers in the U.S. we are quick to label as deficient. What is the difference? Color and culture.

The United States has made ethnicity a political issue as much as it is a cultural identity. In one sense, the debates about cultural politics have been defining events for public intellectuals. University campuses have found themselves cloaked within the political identity that the vigor and publicity its contemporary cultural studies debates determine. However, these issues of culture, community politics, and social policy are not contemporary academic issues. A school of intellectual thought devoted to the study of the intersections between language, thought, and culture has been a historical fact of life in academe. It was certainly a part of my education as a linguist. I do not recall a textbook on issues of language and society that did not have a required chapter on "Language, Thought, and Culture." But when one of the defining phenomena of life in the United States included the politicization of cultures, the intriguingly shared spaces between language and thought and their associations with culture became dangerous territories for social theorists (who only wanted to theorize in private, ivory-towered academic arenas) to negotiate. The shift from classroom to political communities was neither easily nor comfortably negotiated.

Linguistic philosophers have not generally been known for a particularly bold scholarship that asserts a public identity for itself outside of academe. Attentive to late twentieth-century very public policy debates surrounding cultural issues, linguists adopted a cautious stance regarding an association between the three. As a consequence, the special discretion and boldness that are required to explore relationships between thinking, culture, and language, and the relationship of these determinations to public policy issues, have been largely avoided.

Law professor Mari Matsuda has argued issues of law and language as they appear in adversarial environments. Critical race theorizing in legal environments runs counter to political policies that argue economic class as a firmer territory for legislation than cultural identity. Matsuda's point, that "If language is the nest of culture and cultural diversity is an absolute good then linguistic tolerance is a legitimate end of the law," does not find an uncontested space in our communities. [7]

America's linguistic prejudices are intransigent and demeaning. By and large, they resist the kind of academic insights linguists provide about language and dialect equity. Linguists mostly talk to each other anyway. And when we do venture out into the public school arenas, our presence is usually restricted to teacher in-service meetings held at the beginning of a school year. We rarely talk to parents whose children are using the language we theorize about over coffee and bagels. When I taught public school, I remember busily incorporating the latest linguistic theory into my inner city classrooms. We had long and lively debates in my eighth grade language arts classroom about "school talk" and "home talk." I valiantly supported the worthiness of each child's language. I nurtured their nonstandard dialects as valuable and important. And then, Sharon's mother came to see me wanting to know what kind of nonsense I was trying to teach her daughter. I want her to talk the kind of English that is going to get her into college and get her a job and career, she said. She had left work early to get to the school so she could talk to me before my day ended at 3:30 P.M. Where do you think all of this bad grammar is going to get her? Where you are? Public school teaching, I learned, was a real world place where I would be held immediately responsible for my intellectual ideologies. Failing the reality check, I enrolled in graduate school and retreated to the ideological safe haven of a university campus. Here, Sharon's mother could be an abstraction and would not visit me during my planning hour.

Our national prejudice and ignorance about language differences in ethnic or regional speech communities is yet today a shared assumption that speakers in some communities and of certain ethnicities speak impoverished dialects that reflect both an impoverished culture and impoverished thinking. The great majority of linguists have effectively withdrawn from these potentially bruising public debates. Partly as a consequence of our low public profiles, the collaborative relationship between attitudes about language, thought, and culture, and the behaviors that racism and prejudice provoke, have not diminished.

Public art—I mean consumer art forms especially like music and film—documents with fascinating clarity, and some degree of thoughtfulness, the potential relationships between what we say, what we think about, and the way cultural codes regulate those processes. Many times, this artistry parallels our lives, representing in creative but nonetheless disturbingly familiar images the realities of our contemporary lives. One of the reasons Spike Lee's film *Do the Right Thing* encountered as much criticism as it did was its recognizability. Its issues, the neighborhood, and its tensions were familiarly contested grounds. Especially resonant to me were the ways that Lee's film acknowledged the linguistic features of bias that intersperse all ethnic communities in the United States.[8]

The movie's text foregrounds the relationship between linguistic (cultural) difference and the anger and rage that cultural (linguistic) intolerance provokes. For example, Mookie (the character Lee plays in this movie) shouts abusively at the Puerto Rican mother of his son when her vexation at his inattention to the two of them is rendered in an irritated monologue. It is not that Mookie has not been able to ignore Tina's other outbursts in this scene. What is intolerable to him about this encounter is that this particular diatribe provokes a response from the baby's grandmother—in Spanish. Mookie's frustrated response is: "English! English! I want my son to speak English!"

Mookie's anxiety echoes a contemporary conservative sentiment of late twentieth-century politics. We find it expressed across the United States as black urban communities face increasingly large immigrant populations whose first language is not English. The contemporary color of the "face" of this debate has challenged the easy integration of these contemporary neighborhoods. Linking the destructive biases of color prejudice to the troubling manifestations of linguistic prejudice complicates the already volatile political and economic differences within urban neighborhoods like the one represented in Lee's film. Although the reality of prejudice is that it is a reductive and simplistic ideology, Lee forces the text of *Do the Right Thing* to indicate the degree to which a superficial construct can still provoke and initiate real damage.

Because the majority of late twentieth-century immigrants are people of color, a formerly passive sociolinguistic event—the common and ordinary evolution into English language competency of immigrant populations in United States history—has evolved into an aggressively political campaign pitting contemporary immigrant communities against established African American neighborhoods. Language and color coalesce to inscribe the prejudice ready to emerge when ethnicity and color are (even superficially) paired. Toni Morrison ponders the weight of this association as it cultivates a kind of *race talk* that is an

> explicit insertion into everyday life of racial signs and symbols that have no meaning other than pressing African Americans to the lowest level of the racial hierarchy. Popular culture, shaped by film, theater, advertising, the press, television and literature, is heavily engaged in race talk. It participates freely in this most enduring and efficient rite of passage into American culture: negative appraisals of the native-born black population. Only when the lesson of racial estrangement is learned is assimilation complete. *Whatever the lived experience of immigrants with African Americans—pleasant, beneficial or bruising—the rhetorical experience renders blacks as noncitizens, already discredited outlaws.* (Emphasis added)[9]

As if to illustrate this dangerous coalition of biases, angry and violent incidents in Lee's movie are consistently linked to the linguistic agency of spoken language and are scattered throughout, both within and without of the several ethnic (and speech) communities that Lee features. They include a youth who has potential power not only because he is a male but because of his light (near-to-white) skin.[10] However, Smiley's verbal handicap—he stutters—destabilizes these potentially empowering identities. His appearances in Lee's film are coupled to his frustrated efforts to sell postcard-sized photographs of Malcolm X and Martin Luther King. Smiley's venture is largely unsuccessful because his language disability—he cannot competently articulate the text of his postcards—prevents him from making an effective sale. We are also encouraged here to consider the possibility that these two philosophies (confrontation and non-violence) are irreconcilable. It is as if the stutter disables their conversation as well, because no dialogue effectively negotiated the extremes of ideology Malcolm and King represented. Lee skillfully relates the discomfort and agitation that stuttering arouses in its listeners to the tension and irritation that have come to accompany linguistic, and finally, cultural difference. At the same time, he allows a stutter to represent the disabled conversation between King and Malcolm X.

An ethnic mix of English words and Italian grammar and phonology make a loud and insistent claim on the scenes involving Sal, an Italian American father, and his two sons, Pino and Vito. Consequently, the tension and anger that accompany their presence in the black neighborhood are linked to the way they sound as much as it is related to the economic disempowerment they represent. The urban-Brooklyn configuration of their Italian accents agitates and underscores what is actually the more powerful emblem of their difference—the restaurant, an occupied space that indicates their economic entitlement as (white) businessmen. Even considering this separation of powers between them and the black community where their restaurant is located, it is the loud echo of their voices that troubles the underbelly of each scene and that finally provokes the incipient violence.

The Korean grocers are also economically empowered "others" in this film. And their language too is a site of conflict. In one scene, Radio Raheem—large, dark, and loud— looms over the small Asian grocer and his wife, vociferously protesting their minimal command of English, even correcting their pronunciation. But the subtextual juxtaposition belies his size, volume, and English-language facility. Despite the visual's dynamics and the volume's mechanics, because they are shopowners, the Koreans are the ones with real power. Radio's efforts to assert his physical self over them succeeds visually and verbally but not, we know, substantively.

Lee's films have a history of privileging intimate, constant conversation and persistent chatter that seem to have little functional (plot-centered) purpose. In *Do the Right Thing*, this technique serves to solidify the diverse ethnicities and to reinforce the geographical locus of his characters. Even the visual language of graffiti—"Tawana (Brawley) Told the Truth"—that instantiates a written text onto the film's scenes recalls the racialized violence of her real-life experience in Wappinger Falls, New York. Each of these linguistic events, whether it appears as script or voice, is connected to the film's text of violence, power, and agency—an association introduced in Rosie Perez's opening urban dance to the lyrics of Public Enemy's rap "Fight the Power." As *Do the Right Thing* ends, Smiley, whose stuttering has disabled any verbal articulation of the relationship between King and Malcolm X, tapes a ragged remnant of their postcard to the burned wall of the restaurant that once showcased photographs of famous Italians. Sal's place is trashed and destroyed during the riot that follows his altercation with Radio Raheem and his "ghetto blaster." Mookie initiates this event when he angrily throws a garbagecan through the restaurant's window, incensed that policemen have killed Radio in their response to a call about the restaurant dispute.

Highlighting the paired intimacy between language

and violence is the fact that the altercation itself begins with Sal's insistence that Radio cannot play the loud, intrusive rhythms of African American rap in his Italian restaurant—a defense of the ethnically pure economic territory that he and his sons marginally maintain in the midst of the 'hood. As the crowd's anger and violence threaten to overwhelm the streets and nears the Korean grocery, the grocers plead for safety from the community's rage, claiming that they are "brothers." "You, me, we the same" the shopkeeper asserts, even as their language, their ethnicity, and their economic potential claim otherwise.

But this ethnic alliance is a fiction, as the actual events of the 1992 Los Angeles rebellion indicate. Clearly, the proximity of African Americans and Koreans is an explosive territory. In South Central L.A., there was little evidence of the kinship claimed in Lee's movie. The economic breach that Korean entrepreneurship in African American neighborhoods represented proved a volatile space. The clash of customs and language, coupled with the disparity of economic potential, made it even less likely that the chasm between these two cultures could be bridged.

In Lee's movie, there are few spoken words left to bridge the chasm of the night's violence. The walled graffiti, silently proclaiming Tawana Brawley's failed truth, frames the dismal remnants of a night's riot. This image superimposes itself over the audience's memory of the earlier scene of the originally clean and secure street—full of chatty neighbors and the noisiness of urban discourse. And finally, the written text of Martin Luther King's and Malcolm X's words somberly scroll across the screen in a linguistic juxtaposition to the photograph the stuttering Smiley could not explain.

Lee chooses a shared text from their histories—violence—and allows the contesting postures of their words to speak the complicated message of his film. To King's declaration that "Violence creates bitterness in the survivors and brutality in the destroyers" is Malcolm's response that "I don't call it violence when it's self defense. I call it intelligence." Both of these, Lee insists, not one or the other, contain the text of his film.

If linguists were to assert the associations between language, culture, and thought that our social lives indicate are viable, we must also engage the text of violent activism these issues encounter. Cultural issues like the one fictionalized into Lee's movie have generated turbulent conflicts. We academic linguists have been consistent in our arguments that there are no culturally poor people (only cultures at a disadvantage) and no cultures who think less or less well than others (only thinkers who are thought less of). But, when coupled to the abusive contradictions that the reductive tendencies of all prejudice, and specifically the reductive arguments of linguistic prejudices, encourage, academic assertiveness loses its force. [11] It has no counter to Morrison's claim in "On the Backs of Blacks" that a "hostile posture toward resident blacks must be struck at the Americanizing door before it will open." [12]

Perhaps in recognition of the hostility, linguists have found it safer to retreat from public discussions of the associations between language, thought, and culture that are empirically defensible and intellectually intriguing. Instead of making it clear why talking and thinking, although surely related, must not be confused with each other, linguists' passive academic postures sustain by default prejudicial language stereotypes. The comparatively passive scholarly debate falters before the aggressive abuse of prejudice. Rules of polite encounter that generally negotiate usually private academic disagreements deflate when they meet the aggressive public politics of the street. The unchallenged valuation of monoculturalism results from our disciplinary silence.

Precious Expression

I too have been guilty of this silence. My silence was preceded by an early career surge of energy directed toward classes, conferences, and essays in which I argued and asserted, and testified and taught against the research biases that linked competence (what we know) and expressive language (how we say it). My objective was to dismantle the cultural biases that disabled the performances of black children who spoke nonstandard dialects in our nation's classrooms. Too many teachers did not understand that the way their children talked had nothing whatsoever to do with their ability to learn to read and write. [13] However, children's abilities to learn literacy *were* significantly affected by their teachers' biases.

In isolation, as a linguistic principle, the link between competence and performance is not a problematic notion to consider. [14] However, racist notions that some dialects, like some people, are smarter and better than others sustain ethnic prejudice in the United States. (On a global level, language prejudices are revealed when most of us support the idea that some languages are romantic and lovely, and others are harsh and brutal. And, when we are asked which people of the world are most romantic, and which are the least sensitive and caring, our answers match the prejudices of our language biases.)

The constant argumentativeness invoked by my efforts to disable these linguistic biases was finally too difficult for me to sustain. Too many held on too resolutely to their dangerous belief that lower class and black speakers use a "restricted" language—where ideas, reasoning ability, and sentence length are equally abbreviated.[15] The unchanging dimensions of this issue grew tiresome and familiar. I heard some version of the following refrain one too many times: "But if they (meaning African American children) don't speak clearly (meaning standard English), then they can't be thinking clearly." The fact that both research and empirical evidence (my own and other academic linguists') clearly supported the fact that a child's expressive language—whether a standard or nonstandard dialect—had absolutely nothing to do with potential for literacy failed to impress its reason upon too many teachers' persistent prejudices about the viability of this association.

This nation's overwhelmingly powerful (albeit indefensible) judgment that there are indeed intelligent speech patterns spoken by smart (and white) people and deficient speech patterns used by ignorant (and black) people continues to constrict the potential of African American children—especially if their dialects are nonstandard. Every semester, as I was asked to lead workshops, participate in research seminars, write, and teach classes in "language in society" and "American dialects," I wondered with mounting frustration how many times and for how many years I would have to confront this same, tired history of language prejudice.

The focus of my research and teaching was especially difficult because I was absolutely convinced that if I were not vigilant, that prejudice could easily disable my own potential. I knew that all I would have to do would be to enter one of those seminars or lead one of those classes or in-service workshops using a "nonstandard," black-identified urban dialect and my credibility would be washed away. Even if we all had reached a scholarly and intellectual agreement that dialects are relevant to culture but not reflective of competence,

I was painfully aware that centuries of social attitudes that link color and dialect would have more power and relevance than any intellectual commitment my lectures and presentations could provoke. Because color prejudices are so ingrained in America, when color *and* language are linked, those prejudices are linked as well.

For example, when America got to both see and hear Joycelyn Elders, Clinton's candidate for the post of surgeon general, we also got the opportunity to see the activity of racism linked to linguistic bias. One of the reasons a U.S. senator felt licensed to label Joycelyn Elders as a "foolish woman" was not only the content of her speech, but its manner. Elders's dialect retains some of the nonstandard features that identify her region and ethnicity. Her assertiveness on children's health issues offended the sensitivities of conservative politicos. In more than one nationally broadcast speech, Elders insisted that we teach America's youth what to do in the back seat as we teach them, in driver's education, what to do in the front seat. Elders's sentiments about sex education were powerful enough antagonists; but what encouraged her easy and disrespectful targeting were the dialect codes in her speech that separated her from the standardized mainstream.

Whatever policy disagreements the Senate had with (failed) Clinton nominees Lani Guinier (as deputy attorney general for civil rights) or Zoe Baird or Kimba Wood (as attorney general), it would have been unthinkable to speak so disrespectfully of them in public. In December of 1993, when Elders speculated that legalization of some drugs could lead to a reduction in urban crime, Reagan-era Secretary of Education William Bennett felt no compunction calling her "nutty" on a C-SPAN call-in show. During the same interview with Charles Lamb, Bennett easily acknowledged that conservative pundit William Buckley had expressed the same

Surgeon General Joycelyn Elders and her predecessors testify before the House Subcommittee on Health and the Environment, February 7, 1994. AP/ Wide World Photos

sentiment as Elders's. Buckley was merely "mistaken" in his view, according to Bennett. Elders, he repeated, was "simply nutty."[16] The standard linguistic behavior of Clinton's failed nominees saved them from the verbal abuse Surgeon General Elders experienced during her confirmation hearings. Elders's dialect continues to make her vulnerable to the public abuse that Bennett's offensive comment typifies. The November 1994 elections made Clinton's administration less interested in looking (or sounding) like America. In December Bill Clinton fired Joycelyn Elders. The justification? A statement she had *never* made—that schools should teach children how to masturbate. She had actually said, at an AIDS conference, that masturbation was part of human sexuality and therefore part of what should be taught in schools, that ignorance hadn't worked. How and why could Clinton ignore the easily available public record of her comment? Elders's "plain-spoken" style was her downfall. When Clinton went along with the deliberate misrepresentation of her words, he displayed the intellectually dishonest and disrespectful conduct that an assertive ethnicity earns.

A similar example can be seen in a *Time* magazine story that reported on the national attention directed toward the senior aide of Louis Farrakhan, Khalid Abdul Muhammad.[17] Muhammad had delivered a speech to a gathering of students at Kean College in New Jersey. When *Time* reported on the pressure "black leaders across the U.S." were experiencing to condemn this speech, Muhammad's comments were printed with a graphic representation of his dialectal inflection. Included among his slurs, *Time* reported, was his name calling— "bagel-eatin', lox-eatin' "—among them.

Linguistically, this was a very strange piece of journalism. Among the many thousands of Americans whose pronunciations of the final "ing" in progressive verbs inflect the sound in exactly the same way as did Khalid Muhammad (so it sounds like "in" not "eng"), journalistic coverage of their remarks do not, as a matter of course, include the diacritical representation of the speaker's dialect. The only reason the authors of this essay included those features was to underscore the racial line the story was reportin'. It was race talk—an insertion of a racial sign with no other intent but to connect this man's thought with his culture and, in the process, denigrate them both. Those marks helped the argument the article advanced—that "there's . . . a slow burn of controversy . . . exploding into the kind of racial brush fire that's become familiar in American political discourse . . . a semi-obscure black figure says something outrageous or anti-Semitic . . . [and] black leaders are forced to condemn the offending words and the offensive speaker."[18] The printed text of Muhammad's comments played on the low esteem with which black dialectal features are held in the United States. The features would help the reader condemn both the "offending words" *and* the "offensive speaker," establishing the tried and true ethnic connection that would link our well-worn and sure dialect prejudices with a black identity. *Time's* not-so-subtle journalistic persuasion plays on the ethics/ethnicity relationship in a shameful way.

Like many African Americans, I am bi-dialectal—proficient in both standard (acultural) English and in a dialect that identifies my ethnic community. As an academic linguist and an African American woman, my public (academic) performances about what was essentially my private (community-based) identity were schizophrenic nightmares. Even though my physical appearance—the fact of my dark skin—called forth lurking prejudices, my standard dialect contradicted those prejudices. Even though the text of my presentations argued their association ("Yes, there are ethnic identifiers in spoken language"), at the same time it would argue their irrelevance ("No, these have no intrinsic impact whatsoever on literacy, learning, or intelligence"). Even though I spoke about nonstandard dialects, I spoke in a standard dialect. Buffeted about by these circuitous situations (in which I was on one level both object of the discourse, and its subject, and on another level, absolutely separated from it), it was relatively easy to lead me toward paranoia. I was certain (on one level) that the day I used a nonstandard form in something as black-identified as subject-verb agreement in a public presentation, I would lose control (on the other level) of the carefully constructed public persona that I had nurtured so assiduously and the academic reliability I so carefully controlled. My paranoia assured me that if I, an African American academic, made that fatal ethnic faux pas, it would never be treated as a casual slippage or an informal aside. It would instead be the "Ah ha!" moment I was certain my wary audiences awaited.

I can reach many years back and consistently recover memories of speakers I have heard (especially in black churches), family friends, and (even today's) colleagues, who must have felt a similar pressure because they have developed the spoken standard dialect linguists identify as "hyper-correct." These speaking patterns emphasize and foreground exaggerated versions of standard syntax, vocabulary, and pro-nunciation (either all or some of these). It is often quite intentionally adopted to conceal the (first learned) dialect patterns of a cultural community and to reveal, even to the point of a strained and pronounced artificiality, the (academi-cally gained) dialect patterns of a profession.

Gloria Naylor's *Linden Hills* creatively engages this behavior in the character of Luther Nedeed.[19] When two friends, Lester and Willie, serve as a kitchen cleanup crew for a tony wedding reception, they are startled to hear Nedeed's stilted welcome to the group of middle-class blacks—all of whom aspire to prove the legitimacy of their membership in the black elite. Luther, the president of the Tupelo Realty Corporation, greets the group in this way: "Gentlewomen, gentlemen. Before we settle into the marvelous repast that is awaiting us, pray bear with me as I extend our warmest regards to the nuptial union of Mr. and Mrs. Winston Alcott" (86). Willie, as an outsider peering into the lifestyles of this wealthy and entitled group, is taken aback at the artificial formality of Nedeed's speech: " 'God,' Willie whis-pered, 'does he always talk like that?' 'Yup, straight out of a gothic novel. He spoke at my high school graduation and you know what he called black folks? "We denizens of the darker hue." Made it sound like a disease' " (86).

I remember a lady in my grandmother's church whose

"d's" and "t's" and "ing's," and especially her "s's" were spoken with such precision that the latter whistled through the microphone and her particular pronunciation of the former often caused her to spit. We called them spit showers—an event that made my sister and me avoid the front row of the church auditorium at all costs. That we might slip into an urban and black-identified dialect must have been my grandmother's greatest fear, for she spent her days listening to our enunciation, ever wary for a "lazy s" or absent "-ed."[20] In the mid-sixties, when my sister came home from a high school exchange year in Stuttgart, Germany, her pronunciation reflected (artificially I thought) the British English spoken by her German family. My judgment was entirely due to jealousy and to the fact that my grandmother was so delighted with Karen's newly developed British pronunciations that she encouraged her not to lose them—they sounded so well-bred. Karen kept it up only as long as she could stand the snide asides from me and my younger sister—and that was not too long at all.

Although the dialect pattern of my home and within my family was standard English, my acquisition of the dialect of my ethnic community was a necessary part of my young adulthood. (My grandmother died before my college years, otherwise I am certain this development would have caused her great distress.) Actually, it was a crisis acquisition. Being identified as that "proper talking girl from New York" in my historically black southern college did me absolutely no social good whatsoever. Today, I am certain that the experience of working hard to expand my linguistic repertoire (in addition to my memories of spit showers and my grandmother's determined vigilance) contributed significantly to my academic interest in linguistics. It certainly helped me to understand the strength of linguistic prejudices—of any kind.

Prejudice, abuse, and the bleak dimensions they encourage are all involved in the grim story of Alice Walker's *The Third Life of Grange Copeland*.[21] One of the enablers of abuse in Walker's novel is linguistic and it implicates the way in which language differences in United States cultures have joined biases linked to class, status, and gender. It is important to understand absolutely that linguistic prejudices do equally dangerous work at both poles—the negative and the positive. They serve to affirm biases that inflate character as well as those that diminish character. The psychological nature of language use confirms the intimate relationship between psyche and speech. The troubled relationship between Brownfield and Mem in Walker's novel traces the destructive potential within this association both for language users and for those who listen, with prejudice.

> The tender woman he married he set out to destroy. And before he destroyed her he was determined to change her. . . . He started on her speech. They had begun their marriage with her correcting him, but after a while this began to wear on him. . . . When she kindly replaced an 'is' for an 'are' he threw her correction in her face.
>
> "Why don't you talk like the *rest* of us. . . . Why do *you* have to be so damn proper?"
>
> . . . In company he embarrassed her. When she opened her mouth to speak he turned with a bow to their friends, who thankfully spoke a language a man could understand, and said, "Hark, mah *lady* speaks, lets us dumb niggers listen!" Mem would . . . tr[y] to keep her mouth closed. . . . But silence was not what Brownfield was after. . . . He wanted her to talk, but to talk like what she was, a hopeless nigger

woman. . . . He wanted her to sound like a woman who deserved him.

. . . For a woman like Mem, who had so barely escaped the 'culture of poverty,' a slip back into that culture was the easiest thing in the world. First, to please her husband, and then because she honestly could not recall her nouns and verbs and plurals and singulars, Mem began speaking once more in her old dialect. The starch of her speech simply we ~t out of her and what came out of her mouth sagged . . . flat and ugly, like a tongue broken and trying to mend itself from desperation. (80–82)

Lest we relinquish the painful anguish of Mem's abuse to the salve of its being a fiction, Walker adds an afterword to this novel, noting specifically that: "I realized that indeed, she might have been my own mother and that perhaps in relation to men she was also symbolic of all women, not only including my husband's grandmother and mother . . . but also of me. That is why she is named Mem, in the novel, after the French *la meme,* meaning 'the same' " (344).

A decade of research, writing, and lecturing on sociolinguistic and psycholinguistic topics made me keenly aware of the inflexibility of language prejudices—especially as they are connected to our social structures and to our psyches. I knew the data intimately. Some indicated that linguistic stereotypes are so forceful that they are complicit in the below "average" performances in language arts that characterize the academic records of too many African American school children in urban communities. Because their nonstandard language marks these youngsters as less capable according to our language biases, performance meeting prophecy, they do less well.

I knew, every time that I spoke, the fragile territory I

was negotiating. My frustration in confronting, semester after semester, the same unyielding linguistic prejudices prompted my own cowardly and fatigued retreat away from the slippery slopes of these issues to an interdisciplinary attention to the intersections between literature and language. In essence, my eventual turn to writing about fiction in America saved me from confronting the fictions of America.

Walker's Mem experienced the intricate and challenging pattern that the metaphorical semblance between closure and silence weaves. I have had too intimate an experience with silence—in literature and in life—to fail to recognize its desolate consequences. Four years ago, I lost my voice. What began as a fairly innocuous raspy and hoarse breathiness, which friends and colleagues told me was an enviable sultriness, deteriorated over an academic semester into absolute silence. As I reflect back on that year, I remember that my worry began in church, when I could no longer sing. Before the end of a hymn, my voice would disappear and soon the same was true in my classrooms. Before the end of a lecture, my voice just gave out. Weeks of rest, constant liquids, antibiotics—nothing seemed to make enough of a difference until the ulcers that had appeared on my vocal cords were surgically treated. That event occasioned a six-week silence. And I have not been the same since I have come to understand the qualities and the complexities of silence.

My father came from New York to stay home with me. He was my vocal amanuensis. He spoke for me—on the phone to students and colleagues, to company who called, and to friends who came by. This quiet and firm presence who had given my childhood such strength and sureness spent his days speaking for me, and sitting quietly with me, sharing and teaching me his calm. My son learned sign language and taught it to me. My daughter read to me—despite it being clear to her that I had lost voice but not vision; she still wanted me to "hear" the words. Enforced by a childhood of stories told—in twilight hours on our front porch, in bed, while braiding hair or ironing—she reversed the role and read to me an exchange of love I can never forget. My children and my father allowed their spoken words to heal my silent spirit.

This forced interiority, worrisome as it was (for weeks I had no idea whether or not the surgery would be effective), was among the most noisy times of my life—and it was also the most lonely. I thought that it had been an instructive period, one in which I got a lot of writing done, and more thinking accomplished, and one in which I learned to listen to myself, and those around me, much more carefully. But its real lesson was made finally apparent later, in the autumn of that year, when I lost my voice again—and this time it was not a physical disability. My older sister's sudden death slapped me back into silence. It was then that I first felt spirit-damage. And then I understood what I had read years ago in Maya Angelou's autobiography about the silence that followed her rape—that there are spiritually abusive moments so soul-draining that they steal away precious expression.[22]

Maya Angelou's childhood need for "perfect personal silence" was finally interrupted by a teacher and a neighbor who understood the strength of words and who helped her understand and appreciate that "words mean more than what is set down on paper (73). It takes the human voice to infuse them with the shades of deeper meaning" (82). Mrs. Flowers—the woman who nudged Angelou away from silence—taught Maya by example, reading to her in a "voice [that] slid in and curved down through and over the words . . . nearly singing. . . . Her sounds . . . cascading gently . . ." (84). It was a process that led Angelou away from her perfectly personal silence and it gave respect to a quality of language that Maya Angelou's own contemporary renderings (usually) recall.

The recovery of my own voice was a gradual matter after Karen's death, and, after a while, I was mostly just quiet rather than completely silent. It felt as if my loss were encapsulated rather than raw and open—as if it fell back away from the surface to a less accessible place. And both losses of my voice—the physical and the psychological—taught me about absence. I do not mean the absence of a heard word, but the loss of resonance and timbre. The seductive sanctuaries of silence mask the dimensions of thought and culture that are intimately expressed in artistic black language.

Doing Poetic(s) Justice

Artistry is neither only a specialized arena in the black community nor just a matter of everyday use. It is instead both high and low—church sanctuaries and street corners; school auditoriums and grandmothers' kitchens; and front parlors and back yards. The end of this century brings to these familiar and threatened cultural spaces a particular evolution of linguistic artistry—rap. However, some of its most publicly exposed forms have separated from these cultural arenas and rebirthed themselves into ethnic aberration. The texts of rap certainly reflect the traditions and evolutions of orature within our communities; but some versions—specifically gangster rap—stretch past this history and even, I would argue, past its cultural kinship as it has evolved into what seems to be an oddly acultural phenomenon. It is this process of evolution and the question of identity that are most intriguing to me here.

As rap has become a *product* of black culture, investing in itself all of the political economies that the process of commodification implicate, what becomes of the culture of blackness from which it originates? At what point does rap lose grip on its cultural aesthetic and grab hold of its commodified anti-aesthetic? And how do the values of public economies displace the ethics of cultural artistry?

I believe that one particular form of rap—gangster rap—evidences just this kind of productive separation of aesthetic evolution from consumer consumption. It may be tempting to argue that gangster rap is an acultural phenomenon (without or absent the marks of culture), because the vigorous provocations of stereotype have displaced its resonant aesthetic tradition. And although I believe that a displacement or rift from the cultural tradition is exactly what has occurred with gangster rap, I do not believe it reflects so much a condition of aculturalism as it indicates a state of uneth(n)ical representation. Gangster rap is racialized through the public's conferring of stereotype. Rap, on the other hand, has an ethnic identity—assumed through its evolution from the aesthetic tradition that it validates.

Race is an identity that is conferred. Wernor Sollors not only argues its "invention" as a "collective fiction," but suggests this same distinction of invention is relevant for both ethnicity and race: "The forces of modern life embodied by such terms as 'ethnicity,' 'nationalism,' or 'race' can indeed by [sic] meaningfully discussed as 'inventions' " (xi).[23] I suggest, however, that there is a critical difference between race and ethnicity.

Race is a simplistic, political distinction that can support stereotype and prejudice. Ethnicity, on the other hand, evolves through a complex association of linguistic, national, cultural, and historical identities that affirm all of the shifting forces and hierarchies of modern life, but that is also continuously affirmed, created, and embraced by those who are ethnic. It is an issue of agency. Ethnicity is a self-determined and defined construction. Race is a politically conferred and simplistic abstraction that is easily co-opted into systems of abuse and domination. It is the characteristic feature of colonial imperialism as its most resistant practice and most fiercely articulated policy.

My argument about the difference between gangster rap and the aesthetic tradition of rap is that the former is racialized and the latter is ethnic. The racialist cast of gangster rap encourages its abusive lyrics and performances by its artists. Racist stereotype sells and advances both its text and its performance. The commodity of blackness sells best when it reifies the public notions of the exaggerated and simplified public profiles of the racial "Other" that racism in the United States has encouraged.

Although rap may seem to be a unique dimension of twentieth-century experience, it has a historic generation within the black community where its debt to ethnically linked aesthetic traditions is clear and unequivocal. Its rhythms echo from Afro-Caribbean rhythms. The linguistic acrobatics of the best rappers is like versified scat and its innovative phrasing resembles jazz.[24] Contradicting this aesthetic history is the contemporary public identity of gangster rap as a validating stereotype of urban violence. A contemporary generation of adolescents and youths, blinded by the stunning commercial success of a culture commodified and fetishized, has adopted this publicly racialized identity of rap and has separated from its privately generated ethnic traditions.

Exaggeration rather than stylization, and a strained fabrication rather than creative improvisation, characterizes gangster rap—almost in the same culturally anonymous way that hypercorrect linguistic patterns characterize speakers who attempt too hard to separate their culture from their performance. An inverse rationale has lured it away from a private history of aesthetic figuration into a public arena of un-eth(n)ical exaggeration. The texts of rap do retain their link to African American cultural traditions. However, the private artistic history of these texts is publicly subordinated to the hyper hip hop of gangster rap that because it is louder, more extreme, and more abusive, is subsequently better publicized.

For example, the same abusive and derogatory language that caused a group of black journalists to walk out of a discussion led by rap artist Richard Shaw (a.k.a. Bushwick Bill of the Geto Boys) occasioned his invited appearance before that 1993 symposium of the National Association of Black Journalists in the first place. In a question and answer session, Bushwick Bill explained to the group that he called women "bitches" and "hos" because that was an accurate representation of the women he had met. This verbal assault is reflected as well in the Geto Boys' "Mind of a Lunatic," a text that relays a graphic representation of a woman's murder and the subsequent necrophilic rape of her corpse. Had the Geto Boys not publicly displayed their own abusive text of urban culture, the kind of attention the journalists directed toward them would be an unusual rather than an ordinary event. The dramatic attention directed toward the extremes of gangster rap causes the stereo-typing of the entire genre. The most public(ized) moments in Sister Souljah's career as a rapper, for example, were from presidential candidate Bill Clinton. Clinton used the text of her music to argue publicly during his campaign against the ethical codes some rap espoused. It was not even particularly important that Souljah's rap was not characteristic of the "moral ugliness" in gangster rap (the phrase is critic Martha Bayles's).[25] Souljah was an expendable item and her text was more important to stereotype than to explicate. The historic and traditional precedent of political racial stereotyping was a device of U.S. electoral policy too successful to ignore. It is tempting to think that Clinton strategists had to have recalled George Bush's manipulative success as he whipped white voters into a Willie Horton–induced mania in the 1988 presidential elections. Clinton gambled that his attack on someone more closely aligned to the music industry's capitalist traditions than to its own cultural traditions would not seriously damage his following in the black (voting) community. Even Jesse Jackson's public embrace of Souljah and her artistry could not rescue her from the oblivion that quickly followed her brief moment of fame.

Sister Souljah maintained her high visibility only as long as the music industry saw a profit in Clinton's distancing his ethics (and implicitly those of his ideal America) from what he could characterize as (all of) rap's assertive and morally repugnant play for power. It was a perfect moment for the industry to capitalize on the alternative ethics within the texts of rap. The race of the combatants—Clinton and white America on one side; Jesse Jackson, Sister Souljah, and black Americans on the other—was a superficially supportable dichotomy. So, for a necessarily abrupt political moment it was evident that the extreme versions of rap that gain the most public (consumer) attention are more closely aligned with capitalist commodification and political gerrymandering than they are to African American culture.

One example of the fragmented logic that is displayed when an ethnic aesthetic is confused with a racialized stereotype comes from the public censorship trial experienced by the authors of 2 Live Crew's album *As Nasty As They Wanna Be.* This event generated more sales and attention for Luther Campbell and 2 Live Crew than ever could have been imagined had not this text and these artists been paraded through the media. This highly publicized event validated a pattern familiar to United States' racialized codes of conduct—black versus white. The troublesome testimony of Henry Louis Gates, Jr., who was called as an "expert" witness testifying to the cultural history of rap, was troublesome exactly because of the unwieldy product that emerges if racialized production (the album and its authors) and ethnic artistry (the aesthetic traditions of rap) are not distinguished from each other. I believe that the failure to draw this distinction occasioned the conflicted response to Gates's testimony.[26]

Gates's testimony acknowledged the provocation of stereotype—"one of the worst stereotypes about black men . . . that we are oversexed and hypersexed individuals"—in the album's cuts like "Fuck Shop," and "Me So Horny," and then advanced a waterlogged argument that the texts of these songs should be considered as figurative metaphors that would help disable the abusive stereotype.[27] His argument itself was disabled as the cross-examination asked whether there was literary and figurative virtuosity in lyrics like "I was the first to make you hot and wet. I wet you . . . you liked it. Put your lips and suck my asshole . . . til your tongue turns doodoo brown."[28] It was difficult for Gates to advance a credible argument that such lyrics were, as the cross-examination inquired, "a part of fighting for black rights . . . for equality."[29] Eventually the cross-examination descended into a reductively foolish debate about whether or not Campbell's lyrics would be artistic (as Gates argued they were) if they had been written by white people (to which Gates responded they would not be). This simplistic avenue was only available because racialized argument encourages just this kind of shallow debate. Gates was, on the one hand, arguing for a point of ethnic artistry in calling upon evidence from the traditions of African American literary history (call and response, figuration, signification). On the other hand, he was participating in the racialized politics of a censorship trial where Campbell's text was only on display because it looked black—not ethnic, but black. Gates's performance was so conflicted and generated so much discord because of the failure, it seems to me, to make this critical distinction between a public and racialized political effort, and a private and ethnic artistic tradition. In equating racist stereotype and ethnic artistry, political visibility displaced cultural identity.

I remember how angry I was to find Campbell's and Miller's book (*The Uncensored Story*) in the "Black American" section of my branch library. One of those glued-for-life stickers labeling it as "Black American" was attached to the spine, just above the Dewey decimal number. (Your speculation is right if you are asking how I knew that it was a "glued-for-life" sticker.) I was angry because this labeled association in the library advanced the notion of its identity as an ethnic text, which I was ready to accept, given the limited space for "African" on the book's spine. With this book's inclusion in that category, however, I felt the label compromised the potential for "Black American" to be thoughtfully understood as a reductive indication of what is actually a section of African American cultural production. The Campbell/Miller book is instead a public commodity—socialized to reflect the contemporary political ideologies of public consumerism. The radical divide between culture and commodity eventually subsumes the former in the high-stakes advertising blitz of profitable commercialism. This game depends on strategy, not substance.

Critic Houston Baker suggests that "moral panic" (a term borrowed from cultural studies) gestures both "before and after," characterizing the public response to racialized political issues.[30] Our codes of public conduct call upon us to anticipate the impact of our behaviors on the institutions we hope will assure us a stable democracy. They also call for us to acknowledge the traces these behaviors leave on the cultural landscapes. An evaluation of the work we have accomplished must mediate our judgments. If both anticipation and acknowledgment indicate the racialized disarray that characterizes our public cultures, moral panic may well be the most intelligent result.

Ideally, a democracy should easily support a political ideology, and even encourage a specific social organization. But both ideology and its subsequent organization have been occupied—colonized as it were—by what Baker labels as the "reterritorialized" spaces of ethnic cultural production. In other words, our insistent ethnicity in the United States does not balance well with our democratic ideology. We have not been able to support both cultural difference and culturally-blind public policy. Baker suggests the reterritorialized spaces of ethnic cultural production—where culture and politics both reside in an uneasy relationship—challenge those arenas that were once merely social and political.[31] When our political institutions are challenged to consider ethnicity and culture as factors in democratic policy, our responses are panicky and protective. The contemporary debates about critical race theory in legal circles, a debate that sank University of Pennsylvania Law Professor Lani Guinier's nomination to the Justice Department, illustrate the anxious tone of this discussion.

Baker suggests that we read "moral panic" in one light as "anxious moments of policing and control," as well as understanding them to be like boundary crises in which "traditionally backgrounded social problems move to the fore."[32] I see these "backgrounded social problems" as the traditional ethnic purity of public spaces in the United States. However, this country's cultural identity could never, with even the slightest degree of intellectual honesty, be read as ethnically "pure," (i.e. "homogenous"). Democracy's troublesome social fiction was bound to dissolve when ethnic cultures challenged the ethic of their representation. Whether or not questions of morality are rightly involved in these cultural dilemmas, the perception of this involvement is enough to sabotage a celebration of the aesthetic traditions that are linked—in this venue particularly—to rap.

These traditions do have a contemporary visibility. Rap's verbal artistry and its dance are clearly linked to African American historical traditions. Contemporary musicologists might see its evolution as a geographical phenomenon that began in South Central Los Angeles and moved east. Or they may suggest, as does Michael Dyson, its obscure origins in New York's urban ghettos within the past decade.[33] However, rap's evolution is more complex than these contemporary cross-country geographical logistics seem to imply. For example, its dance often carries the expressive motion, sway, and rhythmic emphasis that connects it to the repertoires of African American dance companies. In these companies, traditional West African dance forms are intentional allusions. Similarly, the poetic lyrics of rap recall the versified oratory of early and mid-nineteenth-century African American poets, whose traditions themselves reflect an imbrication of West African and European verse.

Like contemporary rap, early African American verse situated socially significant events at the center of its artistic endeavor. Poets chastised the contradictions implicit within Christianity and that accompanied this country's declaration of liberty. The political vistas of early African American poetry relentlessly revealed the hypocrisy of America's democratic vistas. Frances Harper, for example, was widely celebrated not only for the political urgency of her texts, but for the highly stylized, emotionally demanding deliveries of her performances. "The Slave Auction" is but one example of the insistent declarations against the national text of slavery in this early verse.

> The sale began—young girls were there,
>   Defenseless in their wretchedness,
> Whose stifled sobs of deep despair
>   Revealed their anguish and distress.
> And mothers stood with streaming eyes,
>   And saw their dearest children sold;
> Unheeded rose their bitter cries,
>   While tyrants bartered them for gold.
> And woman, with her love and truth—
>   For these in sable forms may dwell—
> Gazed on the husband of her youth,
>   With anguish none may paint or tell.
> And men, whose sole crime was their hue,
>   The impress of their Maker's hand,
> And frail and shrieking children, too,
>   Were gathered in that mournful band.
> Ye who have laid your love to rest,
>   And wept above their lifeless clay,
> Know not the anguish of that heart,
>   Whose loved are rudely torn away.
> Ye may not know how desolate
>   Are husbands rudely forced to part,
> And how a dull and heavy weight
>   Will press the life-drops from the heart.
>   —Frances Ellen Watkins Harper, "The
>   Slave Auction"

Harper's public presentations were known for their drama and flair—she *rendered* her verse, giving body and dramatic expression to her message of abolition in an effort to urge her public's emotional response. Harper's audiences were often so responsive that her performances in the sanctuaries that frequently served as her lecture halls had to be held outside on the church steps so that she might reach the crowds who had gathered on the grounds of the churchyards.

There is a generational continuity from Harper's cultural methodology to the contemporary modes and strategies of rap. Rap too represents a fusion between oratorical, literate, and musical traditions within the black aesthetic. The intertextuality of rap's evolution establishes its cultural/aesthetic history and identifies the way that some of its versions have separated themselves from this history. Oratory is an essential feature of each of these forms and a history of oratorical aesthetics in African American cultural traditions would include, in a relational lineage, each of the following. Significantly, each has both a poetic and musical expression.

	POETRY	MUSIC
	West African Originations	
Oratures→	Griotic recitation→	Praisesongs
	African American Evolutions	
Versified oratory →	"The Slave Auction" →	Spirituals
Dialect poetry →	"Ol'. Doc' Hyar" →	Gospel
Black arts →	Langston Hughes, → Leroi Jones, Don Lee, Gwendolyn Brooks	Blues/jazz
Black postmodernism →	Bob Kaufman, → Sonia Sanchez, Audre Lorde, Ishmael Reed	Rap

The artistry of West African oratures generates an embellished and creative record of history and moment as evidenced in griotic and praisesong traditions of those nations. The African American tradition of versified oratory, like Frances Harper's "Slave Auction," has expressive and cultural links to traditional West African art forms and musical allusions in black spirituals. In dialect poetry, one can encounter the devices of nineteenth-century oratorical poetry. However, in dialect poetry, European structures did not camouflage the cultural identity of the black voice. Instead, a cultural voice was cultivated as necessary to poetic identity. The rewarded message of dialect verse was not political assertiveness. Popular stereotyping was its emphasis and its purpose was to entertain white audiences.[34] Neither the emphasis nor the objective of late nineteenth-century dialect poetry is distinct from the contemporary foci of the most exaggerated versions of rap.

Rather than the politically urgent message of versified oratory, or even like the biting commentary and critique characteristic of folk verse, formally published dialect poetry avoided politics in favor of caricature and humor—giving life to the stereotypes its audiences believed and demanded. Its abrupt but highly visible life in African American letters was due in great measure to the conflicting sentiments this audience-preferred verse caused in its authors. It certainly gave them a desirable public visibility, but the cost of caricature was spiritually and intellectually diminishing.

Paul Laurence Dunbar, for example, chafed at the popularity his dialect poetry gained from white audiences, who saw it as a validation of their plantation tradition stereotypes. His label for it—"a jingle in a broken tongue"—makes clear the strength and persistence of bias.

Ur ol' Hyar lib in ur house on de hill,
He hunner yurs ol' an' nebber wuz ill;
An' he laigs so spry dat he dawnce ur jeeg;
He lib so long dat he know ebbry tings
'Bout de beas'ses dat walks an de bu'ds dat sings—
    Dis Ol' Doc' Hyar
    Whar lib up dar
Een ur mighty fine house on ur mighty high
    hill. . . .

He doctah fur all de beas'ses an bu'ds—
He put on he specs an' he use beeg wu'ds,
He feel dee pu's' den he look mighty wise,
He pull out he watch an' he shet bofe eyes;
He grab up he hat an' grab up he cane,
den—"blam!" go de do' —he gone lak de train,
    Dis Ol' Doc' Hyar,
    Whar lib up dar
Een ur mighty fine house on ur mighty high hill. . . .
                    —James Edwin Campbell, (from) "Ol'
                    Doc' Hyar"[35]

In the 1960s, one of the most critical features of the
black arts movement was literature's outreach to the communities whose culture it celebrated. William Robinson recognizes the link between dialect and what he labels as "modern
militant black poetic uses of 'black ghettoese' language, city-
paced spontaneous rhythms, vivid atavistic images." He
notes, however, that linguistic similarities, a "common use of
language, rhythm, and imagery" do not follow when it comes
to the material content of dialect and black arts verse that
"differ in their views of themselves and the world around
them."[36] In 1973, Stephen Henderson's introduction to his
anthology, *Understanding the New Black Poetry*, emphasized the

way that black poetic language, its themes, and its "satura-tion" (which Henderson identifies as its "communication" of blackness) made the coalescence, indeed the cooperation, be-tween its public and its cultural identity, the most salient feature within African American poetry.[37] Nikki Giovanni's reflection that English language and emotion are not easily reconciled explains the "new" black poets' especially creative improvisations with language as they attempted to saturate a European language with an African sensibility.

Especially because music—specifically song—is a space where African American cultural work happens, the African American musical tradition has maintained a close relationship to our expressive poetic history. Henderson argues that it is "at the basis of much of Black poetry, either consciously or co-vertly" in such shared features as tonal memory, notation, emotive response, language, and structure.[38] Many examples, including the spirituals of the nineteenth century, the blues of the early twentieth century, and the gospel traditions devel-oped from both of these, testify to the intersections between black music and poetry. Contemporary rap, in this suggested lineage, is a fusion of verbal oratory and musical expression.

Perhaps The Last Poets, a late 1960s group whose versi-fied, percussively supported oratory was an early indication of the approaching postmodern fusion of rap, makes apparent how vigorous is this intersection, and suggests the viability of my argument positioning these cultural texts within rap's evolutionary history. The Last Poet's "Black Thighs" ("It feels so good . . . flesh against flesh/and that hot moistness") is as erotic as much of 1990s rap. And there is an entire generation of black folk who came of age in the revolutionary sixties who remember chanting along with this group their radical cut "Niggers Are Scared of Revolution"—a choreopoem whose popularity was matched only by the rhythmically and textually insistent "New York, New York/The Big Apple." The sardonic and biting condemnation in "New York" castigated the city these poets presented as "a state of mind/that doesn't mind fucking up a brother." Behind the drums, the rhythmic voicing of the title throughout this cut worried the poem's line, signifying the repetitive danger in this city's history. The most consistent message in The Last Poets' repertoire is lyrically represented in "Two Little Boys," a cut that laments the loss of our children to drugs, disease, and our neglect. Without veiling their anger, they challenge our vision, "Have you seen the sickness of our people?," and the superficiality of our newly Afrocentric cultures, "while we parade around/in robes of our ancestors," and the cost to our youth, "and all the while there are children dying." It was a critical album for my generation until, as one of my friends recalled (when we were remembering the radical edge we embraced with this group), we traded it in for Isaac Hayes's *Hot Buttered Soul*.

One of the most consistent features in the history of African American aesthetics is the levy that audience response maintains over speaker's intent in this communitarian tradition. A consequence of the community's high profile is artistry's consistently ethnic identity or, more specifically, the dominating questions concerning a black identity when artists—literary or musical—are interviewed by mainstream media.

Although the complexity within the diverse expressions of contemporary African American art certainly includes ethnic masking (or ethnic ambiguity), the fact remains that there are today discrete and persistent ethnic features of black music, literature, and visual arts. A (perhaps perverse) consequence of this unquestionable public identity is that it enables and sustains the historically recurring debates over black language and the culture it identifies. The community's reception of its aesthetic face becomes a matter of the community's control of its public appearance.[39]

A popular (not an ethnic) culture encouraged facets of this tradition to thrust themselves outside of an artistic cultural history. Its rebirth into a public domain where politics, stereotype, and linguistic prejudice mattered more than the qualities of creative endeavor determined, for example, the public identity and reception of dialect poetry of the late nineteenth century as well as rap music of the late twentieth. Consequently, the contemporary rhythms of the highly publicized gangster rap only partially reflect an aesthetic ethnic identity. Neither the performance nor the texts reflect an essential debt to the traditions of cultural artistic idiom or creative effort. Instead, they claim their attention from a successfully exaggerated racialized stereotype that brought them to the buying public's attention in the first place. A commercially motivated public repositioning strips gangster rap from the cultural/aesthetic traditions reflected in rap and makes it vulnerable to a commercial flux. This moment of cultural capitalism in a contemporary, consumer-driven United States validates and rewards ethnic loss and silence. In the place of a silenced cultural artistry is the noise of sociopolitical stereotype.

The abusive forms of gangster rap that dominate the media are not privately valued and community determined, but are instead publicly validated, acultural figurations—a dissonant displacement by public visuals of humping, thumping, thrusting black males whose success depends on outrageous excess, and nothing more substantive than this. If it were not for sale—bought and so(u)ld on the exchange market—and if it did not revalidate centuries-old stereotypes of black women as *"rumpshakers"* and black men as violent, life-threatening and security-disabling *"gangstas,"* then it quite simply would not command the tremendous public presence that it has. Misogynistic rap retains its public viability not because of the aesthetic support of an ethnically determined artistry, but because of the monetary support that motivates uneth(n)ical economic determinism.

The loss of the shared spaces of this artistry is vulnerably displayed now within a great divide that, for the first time in African America's aesthetic history, separates the front rooms from the backyards and the sanctuaries from the street corners. The medium of media, with its ability to simulate the real (in film and television) and to document self-selected, truncated portions of the accurate, has created a wasteland-like frontier between the private and the public, and between the real and its simulacrum. The media's manic discourse fills this wasted space. Whether it is the uncontrollable babble of newscasters, the canned laughter of situation comedies, or the mindless exchanges of comedy channels and talk shows, all share an imperturbable thoughtlessness about matters of culture and art and the ethical values implicit in ethnic aesthetics. Little wonder that the extremes of rap would find such a welcoming territory within this media-generated wasteland. This culturally empty homeplace, signified as the " 'hood" in headlines and movie marquees, is merely the visual dimension of loss. A manic and superficial discourse characterizes race talk about race matters and it verbalizes the character of our cultural loss. Accompanying our loss of character and cultural discourse is a devastation of personal dignity.

Although I generally bristle against the easy labeling that a term like "dysfunctional" implies in our society, I do think that "dysfunction" accurately captures the empty activity within our public and personal spheres. The misogyny and moral ugliness of gangster rap vandalizes both private and public cultures. Our private lives and our public experiences both desperately seek useable values—lessons for our daily lives that will allow and encourage safe, secure, and sure negotiations through everyday matters. But the persistent absence of cultural values creates an unchallenged space—resident territory for the ethically empty economic imperatives of a market economy. Our loss and dysfunction shift the search for useable values to a securing of "use value." Unlike useable values that foreground spiritual stability and moral responsibility, use value is always attached to the properties of a thing and these properties are always, and finally, human properties. As spiritual and moral values get assigned commercial utility, perhaps the most discomfiting reality of all is that all of this race talk about property, value, exchange, and marketability eerily echoes the economic vocabulary of slavery.

Musicologist Martha Bayles goes so far as to allege that a rap like Ice T's notorious "Cop Killer" isn't rap at all, "but heavy metal marketed to white suburbanites who like to dress black and play at rage."[40] Although I think Bayles has the association (to heavy metal) wrong, I believe she has gotten the economics exactly right. An "exchange" market in this era of superficially exchanged identities means white youth can harness the veneer of a popular black imagery (similar to white adoption of black speech as an intentional mark of radical identity) and assume a vicarious cultural difference without ever having to face the consequences and the real-life dangers of being culturally different from the endorsed (i.e. economically empowered) white identity.

Cornel West labels this phenomenon as the Afro-Americanization of youth, specifying the way in which culture is commercialized and becomes capital in an exchange market economy. The final denominator in such a formula determines whether or not the resources—artistic or human—are used successfully. Geneva Smitherman, nearly alone among contemporary academic linguists, has had the bravery and commitment to mount an aggressive and public challenge to linguistic prejudice, calling attention to the abusive dimensions of economic exploitation and, noting that while a "multibillion dollar industry" is built upon black culture, and while the "language, music, and culture of the 'hood' have crossed over, the people have not."[41] Efficiency and exchange value within a commodity driven culture are its primary provocateurs. In this context, the efficiency and exchange value of the cultural codes of blackness have created its market value, as "black talk and black culture [are] used to sell everything from Coca-Cola and Gatorade to snow blowers and even . . . shampoo for white hair."[42] Most lamentable is the fact that efficiency and market values have displaced the artistic urges of cultural expressivity. Aestheticism shoved aside, the particulate matter of gangster rap's abusive composition—the linguistic rhythms, the mostly male imagery, the staccato dance, the volume, etc.—is exaggerated and decontextualized, even by its inventors.

What is perhaps most distressing about this scenario is the easy co-optation of public artistry's intrinsic goals into the abusive ethics of the marketplace. As the rhythms of rap became more publicly pronounced, it bought into the most saleable features of the late twentieth century's U.S. market economy—sex and violence—and blackened these features, reifying centuries-old notions of black stereotypes and transferring these to the contemporary version of slavery's auction block—the marketplace. Like the nineteenth-century black vaudevillians whose determination to break into the minstrel market led them to blacken their own faces in a tragi-comic iteration of the stereotypes of blackface; a noisy contingent of late twentieth-century rappers aligned themselves with a contemporary culture of marketable violence. They have been perhaps only a little surprised at how easy it has been to make money by reinforcing and intensifying the stereotypes of vulgarity and violence that the black community has worked assiduously for a century to reverse, but they have not been at all reluctant to take advantage of the opportunity. As long as it is clearly portrayed, easily copied, and unambiguously rendered, and as long as the stereotypes are enforced, blackness is a valuable commodity.

Lockjaw

This generation of youth has had its entertainment appetites satiated by teenage slasher movies, movie channels that make intimate and explicit correlations between violence and sex, and commercial advertisements that make sexual play as explicit and erotic as possible. When *Cosby* star Lisa Bonet starred in director Alan Parker's movie *Angel Heart*, a persistent drip of blood from the ceiling to the sheets where two lovers consummated their fatal attraction accompanied her explicit sexual moment on screen.

Even *The Cosby Show* surrendered the potential creativity of a culturally responsive artistic craft and style for the more socially aseptic message of the upper class economic traumas its bathetic black family endured. *Cosby*'s family certainly spoke a standard English. Visual marks of culture were left to the Ellis Wilson or Varnette Honeywood prints on the walls of their home. The show's intent seemed to be to indicate a visual artistry, and often a musical one, that was indebted to black culture. Black language patterns, however, would have contradicted the upper middle class imagery that the show worked hard to maintain. One early show is a particularly good illustration of *Cosby*'s subversion of cultural language. When Theo and his friend Cockroach were having difficulty understanding and appreciating the text of a Shakespearean drama for their English class, they finally succeeded when they rendered it in rap—a performance that the gathered family, grandparents included, roundly applauded. Rap could only enter the scene accompanied by Shakespeare—a revisionist cultural aesthetic that was characteristic of the entire series.

Cosby's allure had little success at crossover beyond its half hour. The contemporary appetites of the cultural marketplace longed for more familiar stereotypes—the extreme being the vulgar vignettes of the Fox television network's *In Living Color* as a lamentably popular example of an equally marketable image. Stereotypes abound in this intentionally offensive program. Language patterns follow the exaggerations of the show's premise to the extent that an intensified black dialect is often the medium of the comedy sketches. The most consistently popular black characters on television have been those who played to the racial stereotype and who have sacrificed the ethical imperative of character to the development of caricature, like Bill "Bojangles" Robinson's shuffle along with Shirley Temple or Jimmy Walker's bug-eyed foolishness (properly punctuated with his characteristic "dy-no-mite!") as the character J.J. on *Good Times*. Dialect is an essential component of this stereotyping. J.J.'s linguistic difference from the rest of his family on *Good Times* helped to emphasize his foolishness. His mother, sister, and brother all spoke a standard English. Only J.J. picked up the language of his ethnic community—and he was supposed to be clownish. The relationship is offensively clear.

Lest we believe that these caricatures are relics of a mid-century fascination with black stereotype, we have J.J.'s contemporary cousin, Will Smith, transplanted from an area of Philadelphia deeply reminiscent of Walker's Chicago Cabrini-Green high rise to the plush territory of Los Angeles's Bel-Air as its hip hop talking "Fresh Prince." Particularly offensive in the late century were Meshach Taylor's seven years as the nearly androgynous (but-not-so-completely-so-as-to-nullify-sexually-titillating-asides) foil to a group of four white *Designing Women*. These Atlanta, Georgia, belles recall as often as they can their sisterhood to the old school ideals. Their Southern speech is essential to their characterizations of upper class white Southern women. And that identity makes their satirized, sexualized, emasculating interplay with Taylor's characterization of Anthony—their delivery "boy" with a prison record—especially forceful. His proximity to the stereotype (of criminally inclined, physically threatening to white women, black male) allows their charitable enabling of the familiar stereotypes while they redesign a nineties version of Scarlett O'Hara's genteel Tara. Their southernisms of language and attitude fully enable the reconstruction. This contemporary generation of new black television stars continues to negotiate the same, old, tired ethnic stereotypes and often find the most success when they succumb to some contemporized version of the comedic buffoon that has entertained white America for centuries. Similarly vulnerable to the commercial endorsement of stereotype, rap extremists revive the plantation image of the savage brute and titillate America's love affair with brutality from MTV's safe distance.

Not to be ignored, or even more importantly not to miss this opportunity to cash in on a hot market, the music industry has offered its own version of the visual. The historical traditions of orature, that toward the end of the twentieth century have had their most public expression as rap, have sidled over to the (American) traditions of racist stereotyping. Gangster rap's abusive and ugly dimensions create the media events, sustain the public's interest, and feed this consumptive culture's appetite for graphic, extreme, convoluted, and stereotyped versions of ethnic identity—"pushing what is left," Bayles alleges, "of the black stud mystique."[43] Its popularity attests to the reality that there seems to be enough left to sustain the mystique. In the midst of all of this public ugliness, the compliant behavior of black youth raises a disturbing question.

Bayles's term "mystique" is the key to youthful compliance. Black youth do not want to play the roles of the unknown, invisible, and ignored children that our culture forces upon them. And the surest way for them to successfully and consistently escape inattention in America is to insist upon their control of the stereotyped identity that has been forced on or made easily available to them. Their only task is to make it inescapable. Our youth succeed each time the confrontation grows louder, more extreme, and more insistent. And this point brings me back to my earlier argument about the way in which commodification is a process of both creation and separation—a consideration that leads again to my question concerning the point at which rap loses its grip on a cultural aesthetic and grabs hold of an economic imperative. This question and its context, I think, beg for the presence of Michael Jackson.

Michael Jackson's seemingly inexplicable crotch-grabbing has a very clear and historically grounded explanation that is connected to African American cooptation into the *industry* (as opposed to the *culture*) of rap. The challenge to humanity, gendered identity, and the social practice of inattention to the climate of our children's lives is clearly at the root of the endorsement and perpetuation of this industry's most insistent stereotype.

Michael's sexual identity has been the hot topic of celebrity gossip mills for years. But when androgyny began to lose its marketability in the last decade, Michael responded

Performing artist Michael Jackson during the Latin American stop of his "Dangerous World Tour" (October 1993). AP/Wide World Photos

with a persistent grab at his crotch, as if to announce to a doubting public that there was indeed male substance between his legs. It was not enough for Jackson to announce his masculinity. It was a black masculinity he claimed. Telling evidence of this shift emerges in the order of the films that appear on *Dangerous: The Short Films* (Epic, 1993). It opens with "Black or White," a vignette that thrusts Jackson into racialized violence as he attacks a car covered with racial epithets. The crotch-grab begins here. Once he is violently racialized, a subtle sexuality is introduced in "Remember the Time," where the suggestion of an ancient relationship with a pharaonic queen (played by the model Imam) forms the text of the story. But the subtlety is quickly laid aside in the following video—Jackson's dramatically autoerotic performance with supermodel Naomi Campbell—"In the Closet." Finally, as if to underscore his opening racial claim, the producers of *Dangerous* insert "Jam"—a musical video that stories an urban event with a group of young black males who are playing a pick-up basketball game. Jackson emerges from this musical/visual montage as fully racialized—one of the brothers in the 'hood, whose sexual identity has been clearly established. He does, after all, play ball. Making his cultural membership unambiguous, Michael Jordan appears in "Jam" and joins the pick-up game in the warehouse, challenging Jackson's dancing against his dribbling and shooting. This video brought new meaning to "I want to be like Mike." Michael who?

I think we have an answer to this question if we return to the opening film of *Dangerous*. When Jackson's "Black or White" debuted (as a single film) in mid-November 1991, it featured a controversial final segment in which he stood atop an automobile and bashed in its windows (when his hands were not otherwise occupied between his legs). Public outcry vigorously protested this change of image from the soft-spoken, gentle waif-like persona into the explicitly sexualized violence of "Black or White." And although market forces later compelled Jackson to apologize to his young fans and to cut the scene from the televised video, none of this public contrition contradicted his newly minted marketable statement that served to counter his previously carefully cultivated androgyny. As if to underscore the economic marketability that arose from the public response, when the video reappeared in 1993 as a segment of *Dangerous: The Short Films* and was available for purchase or rental in video stores, vignettes from 1991 newscasts and scripts from the print media reports of its controversy were scripted onto the text as a preface to its reappearance. But more interesting than these was a critically significant change of text.

In the video itself, the final segment was altered. Computerized graphics suddenly appeared on the car windows and storefronts of the deserted alley where Michael's transformation into violence occurred. These graphics—racist slogans like "KKK Rules," "Nigger go home," and the Nazi swastika—offered up a newly constructed *racial* rationale for his violence. In 1991, Jackson had explained the scene as a danced interpretation of the violence of the panther—the animal identity he assumed as the video opened. (He transforms from cat to man and back again in the video, much like the werewolf transfiguration in the earlier "Thriller." Both videos were directed by John Landis.) However, in 1993, this explanation seems to have been cast aside as the racist slogans literally appear, freshly grafted onto the scene by the computer's editing technology. As Jackson leaves the scene of his destruction, he zips up his pants; it is unclear whether he has completed a sexual act or a biological function. The visual similarity of this scene to the cover picture of Luther Campbell on the Campbell/Miller book, where Campbell's hand is slipped into his unzipped jeans, forms an interesting parallel. The ambiguity of Jackson's final act (the zipper scene) is intentional I think, and typical of his unstable public identity. Racialized violence joins the agenda of the new and reconstructed "Black or White"—which should accurately carry the subtitle, "The Revised Version." Violence motivates the hand that seems riveted to his crotch and that implicates as well the clearly sexualized text.

Michael's 1993 "Dangerous" tour was titled with intentional allusion to his new public persona. It was, therefore, especially ironic when, in the midst of his worldwide tour, Jackson lost control of this attempt to buy wholesale into the retail market of sex and violence. His cachet, marketability, and even his multimillion-dollar arrangement with PepsiCo came to an abrupt halt when his image-making efforts were complicated by the even larger story of his alleged sexual abuse of youngsters at his Neverland ranch and his subsequent admission (some called attention to its "convenient" timing) of drug dependency.

The culture Jackson attempted to exploit speaks volumes as we search for the source of our national insanity—the culture of abuse, violence, and neglect that we have allowed to infiltrate our communities even while we stand in self-righteous indignation and surprise, disingenuously interrogating the behaviors that our silence, "lockjaw" as William Raspberry alleged, has nurtured.

Word Work

I come from a community where being well-spoken is nearly a birthright. Where the manner of one's speech—its tone and its cadence—is enough to make a grandparent approve or disapprove of your choice of friend or mate. Where Martin Luther King's wish that his children would be appreciated as much for the content of their character as for the color of their skin was not only a powerfully righteous pronouncement, but a passionate and articulate phrasing.

Our contemporary cultural economics threaten these loving legacies of language. Their connections to the politics of neighborhood empowerment, the theories of literary entitlement, and even to the everyday livelihood of day-to-day prejudice and racism, make it difficult to cherish and remember those moments when our legacies of language left us with a creative empowerment of the most elevated kind. Not elevated in hype or hysteria, but elevated to the careful and constructive practice of artistry, like stepping in concert to a line of verse—whispering God's voice, and even bringing tears to an audience who would feel the embrace of the preacher in Johnson's *God's Trombones*.

The legacy of this emotive performative tradition brings me back to my opening reflection on the way in which Janet Jackson's voice embraces and strokes Angelou's verse in John Singleton's *Poetic Justice*—a movie in which she plays a hairdresser/poet. This is not a good film; Singleton's interest in his thesis is more forceful than the articulation of his thesis, which suffers from heavy-handedness, staccato performances by his cast, and a jerky editing that makes the script fail to cohere. David Nicholson, the founding editor of *Black Film Review*, writes that "*Poetic Justice* is plodding and unfocused and seems to confirm Singleton's admission: 'I am still very influenced by other people's work. I don't think I've found my own style yet.' "[44] However, it is precisely because of the fragmented quality of editing that the moments of poetry stand out so clearly from the text. Throughout the film, Justice's melancholic reading of her poems lingers dramatically over their lonely words, echoing the mourning she has experienced since the shooting death of her first boyfriend in the film's opening scene. When her (soon-to-be) lover Lucky (rap artist Tupac Shakur) asks Justice about the craft of poetry, she explains to him that "you have to have a voice . . . and perspective." Although the film itself had little of either, the text of poetry did, in the manner of its delivery, expressively and clearly honor the African American tradition of rendering.

Lucky and Justice's conversation happens as they stroll through a "Cultural Fare"—a celebration of African-Americana—that is a (just off the) roadside detour on their trip up from Los Angeles to Oakland on the Pacific Coast highway. Just before she and Lucky leave the fair, they pause to hear a group that has earned the appreciation of the gathered crowd who celebrate and cheer the artists' chant: "Niggers are scared of revolution." The camera glimpses this scene from above, moves in just to the fringes of the gathering, then backs away. In one of the few artistic treatments of scene in this film, the camera lingers here just long enough so that some of us can recognize the group onstage, The Last Poets, who reprise the signal phrase from their 1960s politicized aesthetic.

Singleton's signifying is an inclusive movement, collecting The Last Poets' art, the contemporary rap from the soundtrack (including Apache, TLC, and Snoop Doggy Dog), and the poetic voice of Maya Angelou, into the same text. However, despite this gathering of artists, old and young, the violence of the 'hood claims its degenerative space. Just before he and Justice arrive in Oakland, Lucky's cousin Khalil is murdered in a shootout in front of his house. Khalil, an emerging rap artist, dies before his artistry is fully developed or recognized.

Poetic Justice indicates that despite the gathering of artists and the powerful presence of creative words, our community's territory is an unrelenting and brutalizing space. The film makes equally dangerous and threatening ground out of these spaces—a neighborhood, black businesses (the hairdresser's shop), and a park where a family reunion is held. In the park, Maya Angelou's cameo appearance as Aunt June occasions her warning speech about children who "have to think for themselves . . . and try their best to come on up, come on up." And later, when Justice decides to move away from her melancholy, it is after she has reflectively considered a verse that compels her to move "beyond this rage of poetry."

Early in the 1940s, educator and school administrator Charlotte Hawkins Brown admonished a group of girls from Palmer Memorial Institute in Sedalia, N.C., on "the proper thing to say, to do, to wear."[45] Her codes of public conduct were designed to assure the quietest integration possible for black students into public life. They were not only the codes of the Institute in Sedalia. A 1940s graduate of nearby Shaw University, one of the member schools of the group now officially recognized as "Historically Black Colleges and Universities" (HBCUs) remembers a similar admonition from her school's administrators. They too were taught to speak quietly. Women "were expected to be ladies. . . . 'You knew a Shaw girl when you saw one by the way she carried herself. . . . The soft tone. If there were two or ten of them, you never heard them on the street.' "[46]

As a student at Talladega College in the (late) 1960s, I too was carefully instructed in proper decorum. These lectures were usually delivered while we sat in the same overstuffed chairs in Foster Hall's parlor where my mother had received identical instructions two decades earlier. We were taught how to receive male callers, how to wear proper attire when we went into town, and, especially, how to speak. Our near-silence, "talking low," was a value assiduously imparted to those of us who desired to follow in the traditions of the "ladies of Foster Hall."

I think now that the contemporary noisiness of rap is in part owing to those years of "talking low" as a method of seeking equity in American life. In rebellion against the silence those instructions imposed and encouraged, ethnically noisy language, like the unmistakably ethnic identity of dialect poetry, is an assertive effort to insist upon the features of blackness in the codes of public conduct. "Talking low" only meant it was easier to neglect the presence of African Americans in the United States. Rap contradicts that self-imposed ethnic invisibility and gives the lie to the ideologies that equate quiescence with equity. Its identity is, as Houston Baker claims, "an audible or sounding space of opposition."[47]

Unfortunately, the necessary noise of ethnicity is vulnerable to the demands of consumerism, violence, and economic politics that motivate much of American life. Those versions of rap that economic politics have torn away from the African American aesthetic tradition eat away at culture while it slathers its abusive and irresponsible residue over aestheticism, spiritual values, and cultural traditions. Underneath the public veil lie the privately valued communitarian ethics of ethnic artistry which, despite the abusive racialist agendas of gangster rap, continue to respect the celebratory poetic traditions of a black aesthetic tradition.

I want our words to work cultural magic again—to reclaim these places so that children's "coming-up" is not challenged but is sure. Ugly, damaging, and careless words are complicit in the loss of our artistic spirits and the insecurity within our gathering spaces. The cultural practice of language teaches both the vocal reverberations that mark the spiritual embrace and give them space, within our communities, for its essential echo. Its practice is celebration and its recognition is one more mooring place for the ancestral spirits who practiced these words first—and insisted these were indeed stories to pass on.

Coda

Before the first year of Clinton's presidency had come to a conclusion, a taped version of Maya Angelou's inaugural poem had reached the bookstores. The ten-minute audiocassette opens with a trumpet voluntary, followed by Angelou's characteristically commanding voice introducing herself, announcing her poem, and explaining the occasion and the inspiration of her text. The three images that recur in the poem—a rock, a river, and a tree—have their source, she explains, in the black American spirituals "No Hiding Place Down Here," "Deep River," "Down by the Riverside," and "I Shall Not Be Moved." Then, she sings them! Her powerful alto voice draws me down by the rock, lulls me by the deep riversides, and steadies my posture like the tree that shall not be moved. For days after I first heard the recording, these songs echoed throughout each moment, accompanying me with their tones and filling me with their spirit.

It is, finally, the soul-stirring moment we had anticipated at the inauguration. Moved, perhaps, by the passion of the spirituals, her reading of the poem gathers the feeling and expression of the songs into her voice; by the time her reading concludes, the cultural expressivity we knew Angelou's well-practiced aesthetics could command is reflected in her voice.

After hearing the tape, I remembered the day she stood on the inaugural platform—the Clintons and assembled platform guests behind her, the choirs to the side of her, and all of the communities that construct the United States stretched out before her. I am grateful for the revision. Now, I hear that moment differently. It seems as if Angelou had sung for them as well—as if they too could share in the echoes of the song that resonate still for me, long past their hearing, suspending its poetic meters within its musical cadence. The recitation itself grows broader, drawn deeper by the musical prelude. I feel its words not "merely spoken," but deeply felt—the spirituals infusing their syllables with the dark and low tones that toll its story. For some, this revisited moment may mark more insistently the initial absence of Angelou's cultural reflection. Whether this is true or not, it does clarify the promise that thinking fully and feeling passionately about the language of African American artistry is a part of both the invention and the insistence of ethnicity. Cultural work like this makes certain that we will have both enough words and sufficient spirit for the full measure of our lives.

CHAPTER THREE

The Moral Lives
of Children

Tonight, my friends—I find, in being black, a thing of beauty; a joy, a strength; a secret cup of gladness. . . . Accept in full the sweetness of your blackness. . . .
> —Ossie Davis, "Purlie Victorious"

And you ugly! Black and ugly black e mos.
> —Toni Morrison, *The Bluest Eye*

. . . if I stole your luck and your lives from your unfinished reach. . . . believe me that even in my deliberateness, I was not deliberate.
> —Gwendolyn Brooks, "The Mother"

"If she had only given me the car, I wouldn't have had to kill her."
> —thirteen-year-old child's answer to a judicial inquiry

Early in 1981, I joined the members of my AME church in our small Michigan community as we wrapped black armbands around our children's slender arms and solemnly marched from Sunday school to the church service—expressing our collective grief over the murders and disappearances of black youths in Atlanta. Their tiny figures were dwarfed as they entered the massive sanctuary, and their procession on that winter Sunday morning echoed for me, back to the decades-old anti-war and civil rights marches through our nation's capital and our community's streets.

Like countless other African American communities across the nation, we had chosen our children as a visible symbol that would forge a bond with their sisters and brothers in Atlanta—the missing and lost and murdered children who were victims of a vicious serial killer. Earlier civil rights demonstrators joined hands and voices, and Vietnam protestors wore metal bracelets, linking their political solidarity across the United States. Nothing so precious or still was worn by our children. Flimsy black cloth tied over their Sunday school wear marked them as kin to the victims in Atlanta, branding them with our understanding of the lesson we knew they would learn despite our intervention—that being black was a necessary danger in the United States. The event was well-intentioned. However, our activism had a consequence we had not anticipated. It collected our children into a community of victims.

Atlanta's inner-city black youth had been struggling to

escape the nightmare of their community. Since 1978, the list of children who were missing from their homes or found dead in waterways and roadways had grown dramatically. Black citizens in this nation shifted uncomfortably at the message this unsolved carnage was sending to us. Despite our best efforts in the 1960s, despite our attentiveness to legislative inequity and social imbalance, despite our newly integrated classrooms and all our affirmative actions, we were not safe. And especially, our children were not safe. Places where dead children had been located, or missing children had been reported, dotted the maps of the Georgia State Bureau of Investigation. Aaron, Patrick, Joseph, Yusef, Eric, Earl Lee, Jimmy Ray, Nathaniel, and too many others had disappeared from the playgrounds and parks and streetcorners. The local chamber of commerce in Atlanta initiated block parent programs among businesses that would assure children a safe place when they felt threatened. But the children were threatened every day a child's name was added to the missing and murdered. Even after Wayne Williams was arrested, and during and after his trial and conviction, the chamber continued the program— perhaps an unintentional, but still a certain acknowledgment that the threat against children's lives came not only from a murderer who marked his victims by their color, but from the color which marked the children as vulnerable.

A prominent Atlanta newspaper described the community's reaction to the trial as a carnival of protests and marches. The display of our children in Kalamazoo had a similarly macabre, carnivalesque quality. We did not anticipate that our political and communal solidarity, and the way in which we marked our children, could work other than to make them feel wanted. Our purpose had been to help them understand their membership in a national community of African Americans who cared about our common dangers. To display their kinship to the Atlanta children. To indicate to an urban community far removed from Atlanta that we too were vigilant, and wary. We wanted our children to know of our activist history and their legacy and to feel secure in the presence of their parents and community elders. We could not guess, nor did we anticipate that some of them could feel dangerously vulnerable and could come to associate that vulnerability and fear with the color of their skin.

Although our cause was not malicious, I hold all of us responsible for those whose psyches we injured that winter—those who felt just a little bit more exposed, a little less strong. Not all of our children come with the resilience it takes to survive color in America. And when our behavior helps them along in their adolescent and childhood fears rather than secures their stability and trust, we have enabled nothing more dangerous than their potential evolution as victims.

If we look back and wonder at how we have lost so many of our African American youth to violence and abandoned so many of them to the heartless justice of the streets or the careless justice of juvenile courtrooms, then we must at least consider our complicity. We seem amazed that their violent activities in our communities and their constant entanglements with judicial authorities could be so far removed from our safe and nurturing concern. And it is difficult for us to understand how effectively their behaviors have distanced us from them. It seems as if bureaucratic political, social, and judicial systems are more intimately involved in their lives than are our traditionally exemplary parental, church, and community behaviors.

As bewildered as adults are at our loss of moral leadership, our children return our quizzical glances with accusative stares—sure that we cannot be as naively unaware of the fear that motivates them as we seem to be. And yet, we are so displaced from their spiritual and moral centers that when news stories and photo captions characterize their eyes as empty and their faces as emotionless, there is no sustained and collective outcry from the African American community that these images are not characteristic of our children and do not identify their spirits. Our silence rightfully earns the voiceless accusations they direct toward us.

I see a tragic link between our ritual in Kalamazoo and the violent children and youth whose behaviors are now the focus of intense public interrogation. It is the figurative in the Kalamazoo event that I want to pull alongside the literal national crisis of urban violence and youth crime. The armbands marked our children as vulnerable because they were black. Rather than emphasizing our parental ability to secure for them safety and security, we exposed their vulnerability. Although we understood the insanity of racism, we devised a way to indicate its power. We articulated a relationship between victimization and color that we should have challenged. It should not surprise us that some of our children have come to believe that their color is not only a critical factor in their abuse and neglect, but that they have no power to intervene in that association. And neither should we be surprised that our public cultures reinforce racism. Those cultures encourage the associations that public policies enable between urban criminals, delinquent youth, and ethnicity because these policies are inequitably enforced and established, and because they follow the patterns of well-institutionalized racism in the United States. Whether psyches and spirits are disabled, or prejudice and hatred are enabled, color and character have become linked in an abusive construction.

This association—between violence, vulnerability, and color—is one we should energetically challenge, not encourage. I look back at the event in Kalamazoo knowing that today

I would warn against ritualizing the insidious power of racism. I would instead empower our children to do battle with racism as persistently as we have identified it as a fierce, savage, and aggressive power. I would teach them to recognize the pairing between race and reason as the malicious intent of racism.

It is time that we accept responsibility for the injurious association we have allowed to be inflicted upon our children's fragile psyches. It is also time to take issue with those who label children who have been victimized by inattention and by stereotypes as being without emotion or absent of guilt and conscience. This labeling is a distancing behavior—one that attempts to separate their humanity from ours. I remember the first time I heard someone—it was a Kalamazoo neighbor—refer to a child as being born "without a soul." I shuddered when she said this, as I do now when I read of increasingly frequent descriptors similar to hers directed toward children whose behaviors are so aberrant and threatening that they have been incarcerated or hospitalized. When we label children in this way, we take away their human condition. And rather than this judgment being a way of understanding what they do, it is instead, I think, a means of distancing them away from us—so effectively that we make it clear we can neither intervene nor take responsibility for the tragedies they experience. These youngsters who have taken to the streets and who commit nearly unspeakable offenses defy easy academic labels and require of us a greater understanding, and a more introspective thoughtfulness.

It is too easy to desert the ethical imperative and instead to claim that these children are without conscience, absent of human emotion, and consequently beyond our adult help. Relegating their behaviors away from us is a self-serving judgment that paves the way for us to abandon our responsibility for our children and youth. Even child psychologists and social work specialists whose practices are geared toward helping these children have adopted this abusive language. Magid and McKelvey (1987) coin the term "trust bandits" as they explore, in disconcertingly blaming language, the psychology of what their book title labels as *High Risk Children Without a Conscience.*

> These manipulators wear the mask of sanity, but strip away that mask and their other identity is seen. While they can grow up to be seemingly harmless con artists there is also a very dark side just beneath the surface. It is this dark side that puts us all at risk. . . . These bondless . . . children see those around them as objects, targets, stepping stones. Most lie, steal, and cheat without a concern about the consequences on others. *They have no conscience and they feel no remorse for their actions.* The sickest commit the senseless murders so prevalent in the newspapers today. *And they do it just for kicks.* (Emphasis added)[1]

Baffled, overworked, and sometimes inept and dispassionate judicial experts and social work specialists latch onto terms like these and the nearly casual attitudes they encourage with discomfiting ease.

I am especially troubled by language like "without emotion" or "without a conscience" because so many of these destructive children are children of color. This easy divestiture of their humanity inches, for me, too close to the damnable explanations that accompanied the conditions under which people of color, especially African Americans, entered these United States. English common law and the moral order of Europeans newly come to the Americas saw fit to reclassify people of color as something less than human so that we could serve the economic imperative of their New

World. Slavery was empowered as black people's humanity was diminished. A relationship between ethnic identity and ethical practice became the legislated and normative process of the Americas. Both the relationship and the process are complicit in the frightening and disabling environments which too consistently characterize the experiences of children of color. The fact that this dehumanizing language leaks into courtroom testimonies and journalistic reviews where the difficult lives of African American children are often the featured story is especially troublesome.

In a newspaper series focusing on juvenile crime in North Carolina, one reporter's focus made great and emphatic use of the courtroom testimony of an eighth grader who had murdered an elderly neighbor. "If she had only given me the car," the thirteen-year-old Durham, N.C., youth told the judge who would determine his punishment for the brutal and fatal beating he had inflicted on his ninety-two-year-old neighbor, "I wouldn't have had to kill her." The newspaper noted that "some observers [were left] physically ill" as his confession was detailed in "cold, emotionless detail." In the feature story, the teenager is described as one of those "kids without a conscience . . . children who grow up without normal emotional attachments and who later seem incapable of feeling sympathy or remorse."[2]

The "normal attachments" we expect of these children have too often been revoked by social structures that were the first to abuse them. Where is their complicity in the shattered lives of these children? The newspaper noted that even after the Durham teenager's trial, he continued to blame the victim. Children who behave this destructively are victims too. Something has led them to these dreadful events. Too often however, our morbid concentration and intense focus on the brutal activities that make good press allow us to displace what should be our equal concentration on the horrific circumstances that lead distressed children like this, whose behaviors reflect the fracturing rage of their disabled childhoods, to a moral precipice.

If we ask our children why they lead lives so dangerous and vicious, we are likely to get painfully inadequate responses like the Durham child's. He told the court that he had only wanted the old woman's car—a twenty-year-old Oldsmobile. But more consistent than that kind of hopeless explanation are the despairing "I don't know, I don't understand"s in response to adult interrogations as to why a crime has been committed. What ethical codes operate in these children? What accounts for the numbers of youth who are hopelessly entangled within the law or within damnable circumstance? And what circumstances precede their feature story appearance in urban newspapers' increasingly popular series on juvenile crime?

The children in those stories are the same brown and black children who languish in foster care, unadoptable in a country where white infancy is valued, but colored childhood is a caution.[3] They are the children born to mothers who are only barely out of their own childhoods. They are children whose early years were a journey from one caretaker to the next, and whose abbreviated carings-for taught impermanency rather than consistency, and wariness rather than trust. They are the children whose parents were rounded up in a neighborhood drug bust and who lost their homes and what semblance of family they had as a consequence of parental addiction and incarceration.

Instead of an articulate and assertive compassion, one that acknowledges our participation in the cycles of despair that frame their lives, we find ourselves stunned and impotent, reduced to the same voyeuristic outsidedness that characterizes the journalists who see juvenile courtrooms as titillating storyboards. Making their ethnicity a relevant factor in their ethical abuses compounds and complicates these events.

Many thousands of children are trapped in this unforgiving web of circumstance and tragic event. However, when black children are among this number, something in our national psyche encourages us to see this relationship as predictable, and worse, even reasonable. Angela Davis has argued that we place the crime debates into a reified mathematical realm where the numbers and demographics contribute to a national discourse that categorically criminalizes all black youth—especially black males. Our tendency to stereotype and generalize, and our history of racism collaborate here making a critical difference in the experience and perception of African American children and youth who are caught in this vicious set of circumstances. This difference invades every dimension of the crisis. If we are parents and communities, we realize that we must not only rescue these children from violence and abuse, but separate them from the racist stereotypes that support a passive, benign inattention to problems others see as occurring only because these children are black. The stereotype of black identity connected to the tragedy of experience is rigorous and it provokes contradictory responses: it is an unsolvable issue or it is an inevitable reality.

Editors of the *Chicago Tribune* acknowledged the potential stereotypes their 1993 series "Killing Our Children" could reinforce. A column reflecting on the series' impact cited a letter editors had received from a writer who complained that "Almost every morning there is a front page picture of an innocent black child who has been killed either by gang warfare or by parents or guardians. This image and the accompanying article are very damaging because they reinforce negative stereotypes and reduce a very serious problem to the level of gossip."[4] In response, *Tribune* editors insisted theirs was an exercise in "journalistic fundamentalism" rather than gossip— an effort to prompt attention and activism directed toward the problem's solution. The letter writer, however, recognized the more powerful agency of the series' photo text, which put African American identity on display. And indeed, the magnified photographs, spread generously through that series, were a visually powerful agent.

It is important to confirm that there certainly are children who survive the associations that racism forces upon their tender spirits. But it is also critical to respect the likelihood that color and courage, if not paired quickly and resolutely in childhood, will be ravaged and diminished. No one can deny, as our nation moves toward the new millennium, at the end of a century marked with focused attention on race matters and rights issues, that there are legions of children who will cross over this leap of years physically and/or spiritually incarcerated or dead. These are the children whose moral lives I want to explore in this chapter. As important to my reflections on their experiences is my consideration of the roles that we as adults have played in our children's hopelessness.

I remember the armbands in Kalamazoo and I begin, reluctantly, to understand these black bands as metaphors for the way in which we have encouraged them to acquiesce to the destructive potential in the fastening between race and reason.

But for the Grace

Several years ago I participated in a university discussion of campus affirmative action objectives. I was asked to speak on a panel designed to address the experiences of black students and faculty. The series of speakers who had preceded me charted and graphed retention and drop-out rates, surveys of student opinions, and "exit interviews." But when it came time for me to speak, I found that I was too tired that afternoon to pretend respect to the academic distance the occasion called upon.

Certainly without prior intent (I had a standard academic preparation ready and in-hand), but with submission to my fatigue, I violated the precedent that had been established by the earlier speakers and spoke instead about the fracturing cost of the schismatic role I was constantly forced into in that kind of encounter because I could not talk about students who felt the racism of academe without recalling my own experiences with academic racism. I could not report, objectively and dispassionately, on the experiences of black faculty without feeling the residue of those experiences, viscerally and personally, often with a reappearance of the hurt and anger they provoked, and the tension at having to submerge those feelings, as the formal occasion called for.

My unhappily captive audience had only prepared for an academic discussion from which they could emerge with notes and guidelines that would be filed away until the next affirmative action review. But I accosted them with the anxiety the occasion caused me to feel. When else, I asked, did a victim have to participate in her own redress of grievances? Why is it that black faculty were required to be both representative of the problem and the forces of its resolution? I remember saying that the students whose "populations" were available for our review were my children, the children of neighbors in my community, kin to members of my church, friends of my own youngsters. I had been one of them. When I heard their stories of racism subsumed into a category and translated statistically, I was hurt by the loss of their presence. It was too hard, I told the audience, to pretend that I was not both subject and object of this discussion. I am a parent, a wife, a sister, and a daughter within this community of African Americans. What I resisted the most was the dispassionate involvement I was expected to develop and maintain for that, and numerous other, academic occasions. It had become too difficult to sustain that artificial schism.

As a college professor, I am constantly reading, analyzing, theorizing, and teaching in my professional life. But none of these activities is very different from what I do outside of a classroom and in my daily life. Whether I am reading for a class assignment or because it is an essential dimension of my spiritual life, when African American artistry is my text, I know that I am likely to find my life in its pages or representations. Many times, this double consciousness has been problematic because it has encouraged what seem to be quixotic shifts between academic exposition and personal reflection. But I have come both to appreciate and acknowledge the tension between the two and the energy it produces. And I recognize the challenge of foregrounding the relationship between the academic and the personal, and between public prose and private contemplation. It is not without considerable apprehension that I engage these issues. But the procession of children in Kalamazoo included my own.

When I read as a literary critic, the poignant rendering of the often disabling lives of black children in fiction folds me into its sorrow. When I see, in public lives, the disabled children and youth whose violence makes high-volume stories on evening newscasts, I am critically aware of my own children's vulnerability. And I find that even though I know I could maintain an objective critical perspective, especially when the literary subject is children, I find that I cannot sustain this objectivity nor can I displace my deep emotional response to their moral distress without great cost to my own spiritual center.

During the summer of 1993, a journalistic feeding frenzy overwhelmed public television and print media in its coverage of the violence of black youth. Unrelenting attention was focused on the murder of Michael Jordan's father in South Carolina, the violence directed toward tourists in Florida, and the repeated violence of paroled criminals across this country. Media reports were saturated with journalists' editorial reflections on the factors common to these crimes—youth and blackness.

The coverage was riveting. I watched the two solemn young men—one was weeping, but both were dramatically silent—who stood before the judge who would bind them over for trial on the charge of murdering James Jordan.[5] I did not see the vacant stares that reporters characterized them as having. I did see their grief-stricken parents. I did feel the weight of the overwhelming and forlorn expressions in these youths' faces. There was no emptiness or bitterness there, only loss.

On CNN, I watched a constant parade of youths spread-eagled over police cruisers or against chain-link fences, as northern Florida police sought out any black child with a criminal record in the small community of Monticello as they attempted to track down those responsible for murdering British tourists at a rest stop outside of Tallahassee. One mother lashed out at a television reporter—"Y'all weren't here when one of *us* got shot last week. And look at all of y'all now. What I want to know is what's the *intent?*"

Indeed. What was the intent of the camera's pan as it rolled past her and her accusations and as it stopped to focus on the image of yet another black male child, his feet chained together as he was taken from his classroom down to the jail to be, as the sheriff reported, "voluntarily interviewed"? There is no text for this event, only the image, which in the United States we have learned to file away as the public prejudices of our culture direct us to do. We create a file of anticipation that black youth, especially and specifically black male youth, fit a stereotype of criminal activity and generalized lawlessness. The camera's "intent" is to solidify the imagery and the expectation of a national text that criminalizes black youth. Consequently, it suppresses even the reporter's voice-over.[6]

Language, or a narrative text, might distract from the intent of this persistent visual text. Even the mother's absolutely pertinent question is lost in the collective imagery of dozens of black youth being rounded up to face their own jailhouse interviews for this crime—suspects because they have prior juvenile records, not because of investigatory police work. As I watched this event, I noted the way the visual displaced the text. And I lamented its loss.

I also watched the stoic and dignified mother who assured Oprah Winfrey, as she televised her show from Miami, that her son would shoulder whatever consequences were meted out to him as he took responsibility for his participation in the murder of a German tourist. Oprah's Miami-based audience reminded her that they too were the victims of an unrelenting assault of criminal and violent activities. However, no specially called legislative sessions responded to their victimization. No governor's blue-ribbon committee convened to address their endangered lives. In essence, they repeated the Monticello mother's accusation that when the victims are white and/or foreign, and when the perpetrators are black, the level of attention the event gathers is dramatically and disturbingly different.[7] If our citizenry is not safe, these mothers argue, *all* of us should be valuable enough for the public attention that seven tourists murdered in Florida in 1993 received.

The persistently reproduced images of troubled black youth or dead black babies whose faces and bodies fill our television screens and newspapers displace text. These graphic images disallow our private and secure separation from these events. They stay with us and color our judgment. One especially telling result is the way that black males find themselves treated with suspicion in any circumstance where whites can recall the imagery our public media culture urges upon us all.

In *Race Matters*, Cornel West writes of his own experiences that reduce him to stereotype and testify to its vigorous, racist climate:

> I stood on the corner . . . to catch a taxi. . . . I waited and waited and waited. After the ninth taxi had refused me, my blood began to boil. The tenth taxi refused me and stopped for a kind, well-dressed smiling female fellow citizen of European descent. As she stepped in the cab, she said, "This is really ridiculous, is it not?"
>
> Ugly racial memories of the past flashed through my mind . . . memories [that] cut like a merciless knife.[8]

If comparatively benign events like that one make us, as West says, "catch our moral breath," what do malignantly dangerous racist moments do?

Black males are not picked up by taxis and they are picked out by police for harassment. They are rounded up with suspicion whether they are on streetcorners, public school classrooms, or college classrooms. In the fall of 1992, at State University of New York at Oneonta, police easily enlisted the cooperation of a university student services administrator in their efforts to track down a black male who had raped an elderly white woman. In a predominantly white town, Oneonta's black citizens are mostly campus residents. The university administrator unquestioningly gave a list of all black males on campus to the police who then proceeded to locate and interrogate each of the students whose names were listed. It is despairingly clear, in these cases, that character and behavior do not motivate police action. Color compels their reactions.

Malicious stereotypes persistently victimize black males. They are followed in stores and avoided on elevators. When they walk by, car doors lock and purses are grabbed close to the body. Consider the experience of Professor Brent Staples during his graduate school years in Chicago. Staples had initially walked the city's streets without reflective thought about the stereotype his race induced in passersby. But he soon realized that "I'd been a fool. I'd been grinning good evening at people who were frightened to death of me. I did violence to them by just being. How had I missed this?"[9] His racially thoughtless demeanor was replaced with a version of an ethical activism that gives resonance to Cornel West's argument that nihilism is not a pathology—it is a response.

> One night, I stooped beneath the branches and came up on the other side, just as a couple was stepping down from their car into their town house. The woman pulled her purse close with one hand and reached for her husband with the other. The two of them stood frozen as I bore down on them. I felt a surge of power. These people were mine; I could do with them as I wished. . . . I thundered, "Good evening!" into their bleached out faces and cruised away, laughing.

I held a special contempt for people who cowered in
their cars. . . . *Thunk! Thunk! Thunk!* They ham-
mered down the door locks when I came into view.
Once I had hustled down the street, head down, trying to seem harmless. Now, I turned brazenly into the
headlights and laughed. Once across, I paced the sidewalk, glaring until the light changed. They'd made
me terrifying. Now I'd show them how terrifying I
could be. [10]

As terrifying a reality as the abusive racism is in narratives
like Staples's, West's, and those of the Oneonta students is an
accompanying reality—one not as readily attested to in these
documentary histories. The fact that black youth, in record
and seemingly unrelenting numbers, *are* responsible for an
explosive and vigorous climate of urban crime is an addi-
tional, undeniable reality.

It is both correct and thoughtless to argue for personal
responsibility in these violent acts. If we were thoughtful, we
would have to consider how, for decades, children have grown
up in the United States sad, hungry, and abused—their spirits trampled by familial neglect and their visions blinded by
racism. Epidemic poverty, familial violence—both physical
and psychological—drug dependency, and alcoholism accompany too many children's adolescence. They are victims of
urban school systems where blight, racism, and neglect make
these schools tragically and, as Jonathan Kozol labels them,
"savagely" inequitable. Neither their communities nor public
policies directed toward those communities have met the
struggle to value their young lives enough to successfully
assert their absolute right for an untroubled childhood, for a
nurtured adolescence, and for the promise of adulthood. The
contemporary explosion of violence, in urban as well as non-

urban communities, is nearly overwhelming. And we have to ask why, in the past two decades, our children have become especially vulnerable to lives painfully aligned with abuse and neglect without performing this interrogation in a manner that distances *any* of us from the response. If we have not been directly touched by this violence, as parents within an African American community, the text of our response to this reality seems to be "there, but for the grace. . . ." If, however, we have been touched by these unforgiving events, the diminishing heartache that accompanies our involvement is paralyzing.

Just Another Child

As I connect what some in my profession would encourage as a necessary separation between the private and the public (for me, the personal and the academic), I have reflected again on the fictionalized images of black children and on the way in which their eloquence speaks for the constant parade of silent images in the visual media, and in newsmagazines and papers. This intertext is too persistent and resonant to ignore. Creative writers and artists offer an explication that can encourage a fuller reflection on the truncated media images. And it is this intersection—the rest of the story, so to speak—that I find so compelling and helpful as I struggle to address the schism I am no longer willing or able to sustain between my scholarly persona and my community and familial identity. Fiction can re-problematize the simplistic and flat visuals of public images. It gives dimension and offers itself as a reflective space to think further, seriously, and in a more sustained and considered fashion about the troubling contradiction of the dramatically disturbing yet achingly silent figures of the troubled children and youth within the African American community.

Consider Cholly Breedlove, who raped his daughter. His story, in Toni Morrison's *The Bluest Eye*, contextualizes a personal history of loss and abandonment absolutely linked to his decision that his color victimized him.[11] Cholly's history gives dimension to the eventual reality of his daughter Pecola's experience where her color makes her feel ugly and unwanted.

In the novel, Cholly and his cousin Darlene leave the gathered friends and family who have come for his aunt's funeral. (Cholly had been raised by his aunt Jimmy since his mother abandoned him in a junk heap by the railroad.) While he and Darlene fumble through an adolescent sexual encounter, they suddenly find themselves surrounded by a group of white hunters who taunt and humiliate them, threatening to shoot Cholly if he does not complete the sexual act in front of them. The hunters challenge his sexuality and his color, linking the first with impotency and the latter with a diminished humanity. African American literary critic Trudier Harris's clear understanding of the intimacy that exists between racism and self-destructive, nihilistic behavior leads her to this explication of the event:

> The scene . . . is . . . grounded in cultural, stereotypical responses between blacks and whites that have as their basis a manipulation or hatred of blackness. The belief that blacks are inferior leads the white men to treat Cholly as an object, as if he were a mere brute, conjured up before their eyes for their pleasure. . . . Cholly has been designated "nigger," defined by whites into a reality that stunts his imagination as well as his moral growth.[12]

For Cholly, this situation's rage attaches itself to the loss and loneliness he was already experiencing because of his aunt Jimmy's death. He was left with a "vehement anger" and an "inarticulate fury" that became the catalyst for the violent abuse that characterized his adulthood (37). To understand the trauma of Pecola's life—the main character and Cholly Breedlove's daughter in this novel—Morrison encourages us to understand as well and as thoroughly that both father and daughter are victims of brutal abuse. Cholly's father and mother abandon him, and his aunt dies while he is still an adolescent. What contemporary social psychologists pinpoint as the potentially damning consequences that the feelings from separation, loss, abandonment, and death occasion for children are fictively re-created and powerfully represented in *The Bluest Eye*.

It may be difficult to accept that the grief and the trauma of loss result with such consistency in an angry and sometimes destructive rage. But the evidence from our city streets is compellingly blunt and matches the predictions of child and family therapist Claudia Jewett who writes that:

> When [a child] is suddenly confronted by the loss of a caretaker . . . trust in . . . constancy . . . support, comfort, and protection is shaken. . . . The child may begin to fear that all relationships will end in failure, and to view life as full of threatening surprises with painful consequences that [the child] is powerless to remedy. . . . [A] sense of life's benevolence, predictability, and meaning is lost. . . . He is likely to develop an image of himself as unlovable and unwanted. When he suffers adversity he expects others to be hostile and rejecting. . . . *Children with such histories . . . see life as comfortless and unpredictable, and tend to respond*

by shrinking from it or by doing battle with it . . . the child feels publicly exposed and censured. (Emphasis added)[13]

Especially vulnerable are children whose environments and bodies both make it difficult for them to make sense of their losses. There should be no way to make rational sense of the relationship of Cholly's abandonment and the feelings of alienation it occasioned for him to the abuse he encountered because he was a black male child. Adults know there is no necessary, intrinsic relationship between character and color. But because he was a child, Cholly's struggle to make sense, to force some coherence upon his experiences and his feelings, coupled his abandonment to his identity. Adults understand the peculiar workings of racism and prejudice and the way that ignorance rather than logic fuels them. So thinking correctly or accurately about a racist moment often compels nonsensical thought. Neither color prejudice nor emotional pain have a rational or explicable source. However, child and family therapists suggest that it is critical to provide bereaved, grieving, or aggrieved children with accurate information about the situations or events that lead to these painful experiences. They emphasize that it is essential for adults to make certain that children's reasoning abilities are not compromised or impaired as they try to understand crisis situations. But what reason accompanies racism? What rationale follows abuse? Is it any wonder that the trauma of trying to make sense of nonsense is followed by traumatic and damaging behaviors?

The dangers these children represent to their communities do not generally make citizens generous or reflective enough to consider our complicity in the universe of disabled children who overwhelm our social, penal, and mental health institutions—as well as those who still reside, dangerously abandoned, in our neighborhoods. The memories that insist their way back from brutalized infancies and childhoods into teenaged years often match rage to pain. Although these children's conduct threatens not only themselves and their families, but their communities and this nation, we persistently direct our accusations only toward them and their families and fail to consider our own involvement in their unhappy lives.

There are many families whose lives have been fractured by the seemingly inexplicable tragedies of a child's aberrant conduct. But I think it important to respond to the sorrow and horror of the violence of these children as a community of citizens who own both the privilege and pain that exist within our centers.

The stories of these children are what Oprah Winfrey wants to solicit when she asks "What went wrong?" to the legions of mothers who are convinced to share their sad experiences on her stage.[14] These are mothers of children whose behaviors have become so aberrant that they are jailed or hospitalized—separated from their families and from a society that understands or tolerates little about differences that threaten our security.

But Oprah's query is sophomoric and dispassionate. I see them on that stage, struggling to find an answer to this essentially condemnatory question. There is no good useable answer, and certainly not one sufficiently clear or precise enough to explain away the damage and hurt their children have inflicted. The question is hollow because nothing the mothers can say will adequately fill its accusatory space or answer the blame implicit in that interrogation. Far from providing the stories it seems to solicit, it is the kind of question that distances and one that cannot possibly involve "us" in its response. These mothers are figuratively left alone on that stage, as well as on the stage of our nation's interrogations. They are left alone because their answers are not the stuff of a sixty-minute television show—interrupted by commercial advertisement. A storied life is complicated. It fearlessly names the community, labels this nation, and identifies this society as an essential text in its construction. It will not allow the figurative distance of the stage that encourages our delusion that we are always audience—the voyeurs; because if we are not, then we might be the only other simplistic visual the talk show format offers—the vulnerable object of inquisition. I have learned to recognize such barriers as artificial distinctions between the public and the private that fail when the visual image gains the dimension of text. So I resist the space assigned to staged mothers and audiences—one isolated in their trauma and despair, the other insulated in their security and distance.

In a neo-feminist defense of familial authority, Jean Elshtain argues that "Family authority . . . is part of the constitutive background required for the survival and flourishing of democracy" and that "family relations could not exist without family authority, and these relations remain the best way we know anything about to create human beings with a developed capacity to give ethical allegiance to the background presumptions and principles of democratic society."[15] Elshtain's "we" presumes what is an imaginary equity of class, race, and gender. If ethical decision making is among our social expectations of good citizenship, what happens when citizenship in a "democratic society" is meted out sparingly because one's ethnicity is colored?

In Morrison's novel, Cholly's father rejects him, his mother abandons him, and his aunt dies in his adolescence. The factor of his blackness becomes critical to each of these childhood traumas because it mixes itself into these fracturing events. Cholly learns that the only identities he fully carries by himself—his color and his body—are as likely to victimize him as are the situations of his environment. The hunters who surround him and Darlene "were big, white, armed men. He was small, black, helpless" (114). This correlation promises to endanger any who come close enough to be touched by the tragic reality of the way in which he discovered a hatred frighteningly inexpressible in "impotence" (119). Although *The Bluest Eye* focuses on Pecola's victimization, it is the veiled violence in her father's life, the ways in which he was black and lost, black and alone, black and abandoned, black and abusively potent that make him the first victim in that godforsaken family.

Pecola bears a child as a consequence of her father's rape. Although that child dies before it comes to replicate the dim potential of Pecola's own life, the tragic reality is that adolescent girls who are victimized by the violence of their homes and within their communities and by society's contributory neglect of their emotional, moral, and spiritual needs also—like the fictional Pecola—bear babies who have little hope for a life different from their mothers'.

Year after year the numbers relentlessly repeat themselves. They indicate a historic instability when underclass communities must do battle for health care, other kinds of state support, equity in housing, employment, and education, and then must also battle against our society's deep antipathy and "blame the victim" mentality when it comes to adolescent mothers.[16] Childbearing rates among black adolescents are past "alarming"—the phrase social workers and theorists like to use (especially at budget times for agency handouts). These rates are especially frightening because every increase, in this age of plenty of good academic information about these youngsters, plenty of know-how about medical interventions that work, and plenty of specialists who can recite textbooks full of information relevant to these girls, makes it absolutely clear how likely it is that the quality of their own lives will be sacrificed in this experience. In Lawson's and Rhode's anthology, Margaret Sims notes that "unmarried teenager[s who are parents] represent a disproportionate share of economic deprivation within the black community," underscoring, in her essay, that "the young mothers of these children are themselves hardly removed from childhood—their education is incomplete, their preparation for parenthood underdeveloped, and their own personal potential unfulfilled."[17]

This age is full of easily available information that the problem of adolescent childbearing is one of equity and public policies. Facing the crises the children of children bring into a health care system means accepting responsibility for the inequities we have forced their communities to endure. If their mothers' lives have not already been endangered by their too early parenthood, their infants' lives may well be. These children who are mothers too often practice the same parental neglect that has enabled their pregnancies. They bring little experience gained from security to their babies' lives, and a fractured, challenged habit of their own surviving too often characterizes their experience. Some within the generation of infants these children give birth to will likely find some way to remind society, any who will cast even a dispassionate academic gaze toward them, what we have allowed to happen to them and their mothers. In all those areas where equity has been racially determined—school, health care, employment, etc.—these children have an earned disadvantage due to the circumstances of their births. As it has not become atypical to anticipate that the injured children who are boys act out their rage aggressively in gang or individual violence, it has also not become atypical to anticipate that a disturbing number of

girls among these hurt youngsters act out in a passivity that
encourages their re-victimization.

Their early and easy familiarity with sexuality may
reflect a spiritual craving for the nearness and affection that
our culture denies to them because they cannot be sure of a
safe and secure community. It may be an accident encouraged
by the sexualized entertainments of our popular cultures or a
consequence of a lack of carefulness and vigilance within their
families. Or, it may be an intentional behavior, nurtured by
their own loneliness and alienation within a culture that
makes them desire the company of someone, anyone—even
an infant—who needs and values them. In other words, these
pregnancies are a consequence of both innocence and
experience—and this binarism should frighten us all. Each of
these, whether a reflection, a consequence, or an accident, is
the consequence of our active and absolute neglect.

In contemporary filmmaker Leslie Harris's representation of the urban experience of an African American teenager
in Brooklyn, Chontel (played by Ariyan Johnson), the protago-
nist of *Just Another Girl on the I.R.T.*, asserts that her experience
will be unlike the majority of youth in her community. She
will not be "just another girl" victimized by the violence, the
neglect, and the challenge of racism in her schools and in the
city's public policies. But despite her efforts, the materialism
of the modern world easily beguiles her (a boy's Jeep is the basis
of her attraction to him). Her aggressive insistence on a relevant Afrocentric curriculum is interpreted as a direct affront to
the administrators and teachers in her high school. They warn
Chontel that her "unladylike" mouthiness will interfere with
her college and career plans as it challenges their evaluation of
her conduct, damaging an otherwise excellent (academic) record. And especially, her poor and inaccurate information about

sex and contraception make her vulnerable to the pregnancy that complicates the story of Harris's movie.

In one pathetically humorous scene, Chontel and her girlfriends exchange frighteningly bad information about birth control—if you do it standing up, or on your period, or if you take a double dosage of birth control pills—that makes it pitifully clear why these young people find themselves powerless in such adult situations. Harris unambiguously implicates the public policies that vandalize urban neighborhoods. The clinic social worker who counsels Chontel after she is pregnant cannot even talk to her about abortion—she would be breaking a federal law if she did. Later, 911 will not respond to her call for assistance when Chontel goes into premature labor because their community is too dangerous to send an ambulance into after dark.

The kind of violence that establishes the texts of black male filmmakers like John Singleton (*Boyz in the Hood, Poetic Justice*), the Hughes brothers, Allen and Albert (*Menace II Society*), and even Spike Lee is not Harris's focus. Shootings, police action, gang warfare, and community revolts are relegated to print (newspaper reports) or offscreen occurrences. A particular scene defines the artistic vision of this film. When Chontel discovers she is pregnant, a group of friends outside of her apartment building beckon her to the latest shooting scene just across the street. The camera fragments the bodies of her friends—we see their legs and feet only on the upper edges of the screen as they run toward the event. But the camera focuses fully and completely on Chontel and follows her to her room where she mourns her pregnancy. This, rather than urban mayhem, constructs the violence of Leslie Harris's text. bell hooks remembers that her childhood risked both "safety and sanity," because her defiant speech, like

Chontel's aggressive and persistent insistence that she would not be "just another [victimized] girl," was resisted by elders who predicted for her the loss of both.[18] The consequence of her courage was that "deep-seated fears and anxieties characterized [her] childhood days." Resistance taught hooks to be "vigilant in the nourishment of my spirit, to be tough, to courageously protect that spirit from forces that would break it."[19] Our hope for Harris's Chontel is that she will be resistant enough to combat the forces that threaten her and her newly born daughter. However, resistance is not characteristic of children whose lives are decentered by the terrors of the culture that promises to include them in its reach. Acquiescence to the brutality and carelessness that abuses and breaks their spirits characterizes this disabling pattern.

A poetic re-creation of spirit-breaking forces—those that bell hooks successfully resisted—consistently centers the artistic versions of tragedy in black literatures and film. They create a dis/eased link, moving inexorably from one story to the next, often choosing the youngest and the weakest—the children—as its victims.

Cholly's tragic childhood understanding of his spiritual solitude is like Richard's in James Baldwin's *Go Tell It on the Mountain*; his desperate sorrow comes as he realizes that his character will never count more than his color in the United States.[20] Richard has been arrested because he was on a subway platform when a shopowner pointed out to the police the youths who had robbed him. Although Richard was there waiting for the train, he was arrested with the other boys (who had just rushed onto the platform) because he looked like them. They were all black. "He knew that whatever the trouble was, it was now his trouble also; for these white men would make no distinction between him and the three boys they were after: They were all colored" (171).

Blackness is the factor that, in this country, is the socially accepted label of vulnerability and trouble.

> Richard tried to relax: the man *could* not say that he had been there if he had never seen him before.
>
> But when the owner came . . . he looked at the four boys before him and said: "Yeah, that's them all right."
>
> Then Richard shouted: "But *I* wasn't there! Look at me, goddammit—I wasn't *there!*"
>
> "You black bastards," the man said, looking at him, "you're all the same." (171)

Like Cholly, Richard's maleness is delegitimized and his blackness is the antecedent. Knowing that those two factors will consistently identify him regardless of his own efforts, Richard slits his wrists.

A moral act, this suicide? Certainly by Judaeo-Christian standards suicide falls outside of the bonds of morality as an irredeemably immoral act. But our judgments of ethnically coded and complicated behaviors cannot be generated from a simplistic moral code. The desperation that keeps black children from imagining their futures complicates the codes of moral conduct that otherwise seem so easily articulated. Vacant or disabled imaginative spaces lead to suicides like Richard's. And as predictable as this loss of spirit is for some of the troubled children of our decade, how much more disabling this loss becomes when we find it resolutely attached to their ethnic identities.

Suicide does not characterize the majority of black children's responses to the grim circumstances of too many of their lives. Although the Bureau of the Census does report an increasing rate of suicide for black males from 1970–1990 and a decreasing rate for black females, these numbers seem to be statistically unremarkable when compared to whites of both genders. However, "as dismal as these figures are," reflects Harvard sociologist Orlando Patterson, "it is likely that the situation is actually much worse, due not only to underreporting for African-American youth . . . but to the masking effect of victim precipitated homicide . . . inciting violence against themselves."[21] A motivated self-destructiveness similar to the effect of suicide certainly does characterize their responses. Their vulnerability to behaviors that cut off their futures and that condemn their potentials is spiritual suicide. The extraterritorial spaces that death, suicide, and spirit damage inhabit disable and fracture the link I have been encouraging between events and instances that run parallel—like ethics and ethnicity—even as this relationship holds responsibility for that outcome. Suicide may seem removed from traditionally assigned values of morality and immorality because it clearly deals with the not-self rather than the self. But the killing and spirit damage that our children commit against themselves, us, and each other indicate that there are no physical, *self*-assertive behaviors that boys like Baldwin's Richard can make without risking psychic fracture.

If we judge suicide and self-destructiveness as the consequence of weak wills or faint spirits, or indicative of the lack of motivated initiative and stick-to-itiveness, then we judge absent of the ethnic reality that life in the United States forces upon people of color. The view from the colored within shifts us away from a hasty postmodern judgment that the deconstructed psyche is ethically paralyzed. The ethnically constructed and realized psyche is ethically reconstituted so that its code of conduct is at the very least activist if not stereotypically moral. Baldwin's novel suggests an alternative morality because Richard's suicide is clearly, if ambivalently, an eth(n)ically determined activism.

In this complicated narrative of contradiction, we can understand how Morrison could narrate Cholly's abusive rape of his daughter as a brutally tender moment "when . . . hatred could find sweet expression" (114). The only activity left to Cholly is to inflict on someone else the painful agony of his own existence. His ethical loss, tied inextricably to his spiritual loss, his ethnic pain, and his bewildering anguish, provokes his activism. To foreground the conflicting psychical history that drags Cholly to the moment he rapes his daughter, Morrison embeds this savage event in tender language. How else but to feel and to know Cholly's own painful and pitiful past, can we read with the intimate perception Morrison's voice commands as she reveals this savage event?

> [Cholly's] mouth trembled at the firm sweetness of the flesh. He closed his eyes, letting his fingers dig into her waist. The rigidness of her shocked body, the silence of her stunned throat, was better than Pauline's easy laughter had been. The confused mixture of his memories of Pauline and the doing of a wild and forbidden thing excited him, and a bolt of desire ran down his genitals, giving it length, and softening the lips of his anus. Surrounding all of this lust was a border of politeness. He wanted to fuck her—tenderly. But the tenderness would not hold. The tightness of her vagina was more than he could bear. His soul seemed to slip down to his guts and fly out into her, and the gigantic thrust he made into her then provoked the only sound she made—a hollow suck of air in the back of her throat. (128)

The terror of understanding suicide and abuse as the consequences of ethnically determined ethical activism is that they begin with, and conclude with, the lives of our children.

Spaces of the Spirit

In 1963, four little black girls—Cynthia Wesley, Addie Mae Collins, Carole Robertson, and Denise McNair—were murdered during a summer Sunday school service in Birmingham, Alabama. They were victims of racist violence—a legacy of the civil rights demonstrations. In his 1964 publication *Children of Crisis: A Study of Courage and Fear*, psychologist Robert Coles predicted of children who were on the violent front lines of civil rights demonstrations that there are yet to be "fierce reminders that the alternative to stability and resilience in Negro children is . . . the violence . . . of some of their more injured (or exhausted) peers or elders."[22]

A folksong and at least one poem mark these murders. The folksong's chorus repeats to distraction the lines "On a Birmingham Sunday the blood ran like wine, and the choir kept singing of freedom." And Dudley Randall's poem "Ballad of Birmingham" captures a mother's anguish as she searches the rubble of the bombed church building for her daughter's body "Oh here's the shoe my baby wore / but baby, where are you?"[23] She, like the other three girls, is only her mother's lingering memory. Song, poetry, and prose sear the event of Birmingham into our literary and cultural memories.

In *Song of Solomon*, Toni Morrison fictively re-creates and avenges this historic event. Morrison creates Guitar Bains, a member of a retaliatory brotherhood—the Seven Days—who replicates the crimes committed on black folk with similarly gruesome crimes against whites.[24] Predictably, Guitar's soul is lost in the vengeful enterprise. Like other violent and abusive (to self or others) children in literature and in life, Guitar had been denied nurturing in his childhood—the consequence of his father's death and his

The Sixteenth Street Baptist Church in Birmingham, Alabama, where four young girls were killed in the Sunday, September 15, 1963, bombing. AP/Wide World Photos

mother's unrelieved sorrow. Guitar understands too poignantly for a child the way in which a white man's carelessness with the lives of the black workers at his sawmill is responsible for his father's death and his mother's soul-draining grief. That is the awareness that connects for him race and moral responsibility. In consequence, Guitar's racial ethics are as brutal as his childhood experience and they reify his loss.

Guitar's racial identity specifies the psychic fracture that followed his familial loss and the violent bloodletting it allows to dominate his life. It marks the place of his wound in the same way that Alice Walker's Tashi, in *Possessing the Secret of Joy*, is literally and spiritually marked with the scar tissue of her own ethnic identity.[25] Tashi's repressed memories are finally recalled after years of spiritual disarray, when a film she watches in her psychologist's house—grainy images of little girls whose bodies lie lined up in preparation for their ritual circumcision—connect her to those memories, and take her back to the moment when she witnessed her sister's genital mutilation and death.

> I remembered, as if a lid lifted off my brain, the day I had crept, hidden in the elephant grass, to the isolated hut from which came howls of pain and terror. Underneath a tree, on the bare ground outside the hut, lay a dazed row of little girls. . . . Dura, however, was not among them; and I knew instinctively that it was Dura being held down and tortured inside the hut. Dura who made those inhuman shrieks that rent the air and chilled my heart. (73)

When ethnicity becomes a liability—for *whatever* reasons—we all suffer the devastating consequences. Alice Walker insists we move away from the secure veil of cultural relativism and acknowledge the mutilation of female circumcision. Her novel reveals how this ethnic practice is a scar, a disabling mark that is not different in its consequences from psychologically mediated racisms that make our children experience their blackness as a scar. Tashi's psychic pain and Dura's death in Walker's novel are related to the tragedy and loss that Morrison's Pecola experiences. Their injuries did not happen only because they were children, or girls, but also because of their ethnicity.

Likewise, Guitar's decision to avenge the deaths of black victims of racism was prompted not only because of his rage at this injustice, but because his own childhood pain and loss were linked to his family's experience with racism. His moral suspension happened because of the arbitrary but actual link between his pain and his ethnicity. The Kalamazoo children too were encouraged to understand the dangerous cloak they wore—not just the armband, but the fact that they could wear the band because they were black, and endangered. Our children's terror of their ethnic markings lies buried in a spiritual space. These spaces of the spirit are fragile dimensions. They collapse and conflate the physical injuries and psychological exhaustion that ethnic abuse occasions.

Writers of African American fiction chronicle the stories of those whom Robert Coles could label as both injured and exhausted. Recall Richard Perry's Gerald and Josephine in his novel, *Montgomery's Children*.[26]

> It took nothing more than the clump of his father's foot on the porch to set off in Gerald a trembling only a little less violent than his father's disposition, only a little less brutal than the arc of the whistling black belt held in his father's hand falling with a crack across the flayed skin of his naked back. (69)

Gerald's father, Alexander Fletcher, suffered from a "chorus of crying"—tears of his own brutal childhood. Too much like Cholly Breedlove to figure out and enact his own salvation, Alexander took to nurturing his grief instead of his children. "Life had dealt him a hand from the bottom of the deck, had given birth to him in a backward Southern town, had made him poor and black, and had assigned to him a father who had deserted him" (71). Gerald was the legatee of Alexander's grief.

African American psychologists William Grier and

Price Cobbs suggest that beatings of black youth are an especially damaging reminder of the abuses of slavery, writing that "it [physical subjugation] forges early in the mind of the child a link with the past . . . as he learns the details of [African American] history with slavery."[27] In this context, Perry's fictive Gerald represents a link to all those children in our communities whose behaviors cause adults enough terror that the adults themselves become terrorizers. Our children are victimized by our fear of their color-coded vulnerability as we beat and spank them, verbally abuse, and otherwise violently display our dis/ease at the danger their color imposes.

> His father . . . unleashed his belt. Terror flooded Gerald. . . . He turned and ran. . . . "Run from me, will you?" Alexander grunted. *"Trifling Negro."* The belt fell—not the leather, the buckle. Gerald closed his eyes and lay there, curling his body into the smallest possible target. This beating, he knew, would last forever. This one he would not live through. (Emphasis added; 92)

Josephine, Gerald's lover, friend, and confidant, was as psychically and physically scarred as he. Her casual and early sexuality was the consequence of her father's sexual abuse—a fact known by her mother whose reaction was to label her victimized daughter as a "hussy." A "Black, ungodly, murdering hussy" (271). Josephine's mother felt it more important to save herself a husband rather than a daughter because "He wasn't the kind of man could of lived with me knowin what I knew. That was the one good thing about him. He had shame" (265). Not shame enough to keep him from sexually molesting his daughter throughout her childhood and adolescence. And not shame enough to keep Josephine from murdering him when she finally decided, "Daddy, ain't gonna be no more of this" (211). Experiencing the same kind of abandonment and loss that Morrison's Pecola suffers, Josephine descends into perversion and deviant sexuality that is as grievously injurious as Pecola's descent into silence. Both girls, Pecola and Josephine, guilty only of being black and powerless, find the combination too heavy a burden for sanity to sustain.

In one sense our culture seems poised to understand the motivations of those whose childhood abuse leads them to Josephine-like behaviors. We have invented a legal dictionary of terms like "battering syndrome," "post traumatic stress disorder," "attention deficit," and "temporary insanity" to explain deviations from standard codes of conduct. We even allow for some of this conduct in our judicial systems as we stretch our judicial codes so that they might permit aggravating events like spousal battery to become a mitigating factor in sentencing. However, the same creative invention does not characterize our response to the environments that allow and encourage racialist abuse. No community was ready to hear the deeply enraging and abusive racism that Colin Ferguson experienced mitigate, in any sense, his berserk rampage on a New York subway that targeted whites and Asians for execution. Our effort has been to account only circumstantially for immorality or the absence of ethical conduct, but we have not been as willing to explore the reasons behind the alternative ethics that operate when victims of racism become violent. When writing of victimized children, Ken Magid and Carole McKelvey write that "at the core . . . is a deep-seated rage, far beyond normal anger. This rage is suppressed in their psyche . . . born of unfulfilled needs. . . . Incomprehensible pain is forever locked in their souls."[28]

In our contemporary culture, there is too frequent a coupling between altered ethical codes and negative ethnic experiences and stereotyping. And too often, ethical activism that is generated from the fracturing despair of racism is vigorously attached to abuse, loss, separation, and the "incomprehensible pain" they create. Grier and Cobbs argue effectively that:

> A parent's essential and fundamental purpose beyond assuming a child's survival is to *provide an interpretation of society* to the child . . . a vitally important datum in the child's understanding of his world is the information he gains by learning of the role his parent occupies in the society . . . [the] value . . . society place[s] on this human being who represents the child's only link with that society. (Emphasis added)[29]

Children glimpse our "vicious social order . . . [that] rapes and exploits" them and understand too well that their parents are impotent to address their color-coded grievances.[30] For too many African American children, those whose bodies are packed into crowded juvenile training homes and detention centers, those who populate the statistics of juvenile justice systems, and those who shrink with anticipated pain at the angry rages of their frightened parents, a vicious social order is an intimate, familiar situation. It is unforgivingly predictable that girls like Josephine, black and a hussy, as far as her mother was concerned, have few options to adopt standard and conforming moral conduct. She was limited by her subject position—prone and available for her father, distant and removed from her mother. The only operative code for the conduct that came to characterize her life was that its deformity and difference would match her own.

Alice Walker's Tashi, whose wounds from her own genital mutilation scar her physically, spiritually, and morally, faces the question of ethical choice in her adulthood because of the reality of an abusive ethnic practice that scarred her childhood. The morality of Tashi's adult dilemma—whether or not to kill the woman M'lissa who was responsible for her sister's death—is not the relevant issue. The bleak and irrevocable Necessity of her ethnically and gendered position is the issue. For if Tashi and Dura's childhoods had not culturally marked them, then the Western world's response to their childhoods, emblematized in the trial Tashi has to endure because of M'lissa's death, marks her as surely as the Kalamazoo children's armbands.

The pain of children's living out a black experience in the United States is so consistently the imagery of their lifestyles in black fiction that Grier and Cobbs's assessment seems almost predictable for children of fiction and in fact. They write that "contempt and hatred of black people is so thoroughly a part of the American personality that a profound convulsion of society may be required to help a dark child over his fear of the dark."[31] Self-loathing and contempt are clear and present dangers for children like poor, pitiful Pecola Breedlove who learns again and again, without relief from the unrelenting message, that her blackness and ugliness go hand in hand with her bleak, diminished life. Children's taunts "you ugly! Black and ugly!" so completely frame Pecola's everyday experiences that the one concrete decision she is allowed to make in *The Bluest Eye*—to acquiesce to Soaphead Church's directives so that she might get blue eyes—is motivated by her belief in the pain of her color (56). And it is insane. Trudier Harris comments that the "absence of a moral base in [a] degenerative environment" makes way for the exploitation of the victims in this story.[32] The victims who suffer this absence are children, who either survive, like the sisters Claudia and Frieda in *The Bluest Eye*, or who wither away in Pecola-like despair.

In Ralph Ellison's *Invisible Man*, a group of black adolescents mercilessly beat each other in the widely read first chapter of this novel, "The Battle Royal."[33] Their physical and emotional battering—at the perverse urging of the town's elder white statesmen—happens only because they are black. No other reason boxes them together in that abusive ring, and nothing else—school scholarships, intellectual acuity, or brotherhood—matters more there to their survival of their common assault on each other. Echoing the dilemma of Baldwin's Richard, it is how they look, not who they, are that determines their membership in the ring.

> "See that boy over there?" one of the men said. "I want you to run across at the bell and give it to him right in the belly. If you don't get him, I'm going to get you. I don't like his looks." . . . "Let me at those black sonsabitches!" someone yelled. . . . "I want to get that ginger-colored nigger. Tear him limb from limb." (21)

In Ellison's novel, the scar tissue that forms on the combative children who endure the humiliation of the Battle Royal is ambivalent, as is the "text of blackness" that runs through the prologue's sermon. "Black is . . . an' black ain't. . . . Black will git you . . . an' black won't. . . . black will make you . . . or un-make you" (9–10). When we examine the lives of the children who have experienced this ambivalence, we understand how their making and unmaking is so completely out of their control. Because they must learn to make decisions and choices within the context of such an existential quality, what seem to be the compromises of morality and ethics must be understood not as compromise at all, but as the unforgivingly harsh judgments meted out by the codes of racism.

Curiously, and somewhat paradoxically, like Ellison's

boys in the ring, our children's crimes are both "boxed" together as episodes that collect their race and reason into a diminishing common flaw at the same time that they tragically face the criminal justice system alone. They fight for some recognition that their individual and undeniably brutal criminality does indeed reflect the tragic realities of a community's collectively vulnerable children. Ellison's words—"if you don't get him, I'm going to get you"—can haunt events like the one in Los Angeles following the Rodney King trial. Those young men accused of the merciless and brutalizing attack on the truck driver in Los Angeles, Reginald Denny, emblematize this conflicted, ambivalent text of blackness. They represent both a community's collective outrage at judicial inequity, and the stunning solitude and silence of justice. They stand figuratively alone in the courtroom, stereotypical validations of America's fear of the violence it has inculcated in black youths who are separated from spiritual potential and creative possibility. But at the same time, they are collectively submerged into the condoned violence of our common American culture. Consequently, a literal crossing of the community's border by truck driver Denny sacrifices him to these confused codes of conduct that motivate a whole generation of victimized children.

Indecent Liberties

In 1987, when civil rights activist Al Sharpton, the media experts, the district attorneys, lawyers, the emergency room physicians, boyfriend, and mother spoke for fifteen-year-old Tawana Brawley, they followed all too familiar patterns of abuse. An unspeakable event in this child's life was spoken of by all of them rather than Tawana's speaking for herself.

Tawana had been viciously abused. Patricia Williams writes of the event this way in *The Alchemy of Race and Rights*:

> In late November 1987, after a four-day disappearance, she was found in a vacant lot, clothed only in a shirt and a plastic garbage bag into which she had apparently crawled; she was in a dazed state, not responding to noise, cold, or ammonia; there was urine-soaked cotton stuffed into her nose and ears; her hair had been chopped off; there were cigarette burns over a third of her; "KKK" and "nigger" had been inscribed on her torso; her body was smeared with dog feces.[34]

Following an incisive indictment of Tawana's mistreatment, Williams poses, but does not linger over, the question critical to this discussion. It is a parenthetical aside in the critical and judiciously targeted allegations of her text, but a question central to my reflections here. Williams writes: "One might . . . inquire why the Child Protective Services Agency, which is supposed to intervene in such cases, did not."[35]

What absence of reason and compassion cast Tawana outside of the protected class of children and into the role of media pariah? A *child* had been injured, abused, and traumatized, yet the fact of her youth was submerged beneath the racial and sexual marks of the event. They had more weight than her adolescent black body and they spoke more substantively than her traumatized nods and gestures. Tawana's experience fits into a disturbing pattern of children's lives that are controlled not by their youth and inexperience, but by their racial marks and the subsequent ethical judgments rendered against them because they bear these scars on their frail spirits. In order to save themselves, they take indecent liberties with their spirit-lives and with their potential. Silence and abuse characterize the nature of their freedoms, and whether these are self-imposed or externally inflicted, an affliction of spirit is the absolute result.

Marian Wright Edelman, the president of the Children's Defense Fund, passionately argues for us to acknowledge the tragic ways in which our adult freedoms have endangered our children. Our national turn toward freedom of expression in the media means graphic and readily available portraiture of the horrors of modern life. Our children's vulnerable immaturity is aided and abetted in this explicit liberalism. And those whose growing-up is already compromised because of whatever familial, personal, or community instabilities we have been unable or unwilling to address are especially vulnerable. They have neither the text nor the tenacity to make sense of our nonsense, and our complicity in assuring freedom of expression, without valuing a careful, thoughtful sensitivity directed toward our children who have no way to personally or publicly process the visual overload our freedoms assure them is shameful stuff.

It is morally unthinkable that we should direct our blame and anger only toward those sad, aggressive, and angry children who respond quite predictably to the vicious environments our inattention nurtures in their neighborhoods and in our public cultures without also implicating the policies and people whose power controls the culture. It is ethical abandonment to place our debates about crime within reified mathematical territories, citing statistics and probability curves and baseball metaphors ("three strikes and you're out") when neighborhoods, families, and our children are the ones struggling to maintain themselves within those realms disabled by violence. It is quite simply irresponsible to respond to the documented links between violent behaviors, violent freedoms (like the "right" to own a gun), and a violent entertainment culture by saying "build more prisons" and "turn the channel." Until we begin to interrogate, with the same honesty and passion with which we defend our first amendment freedoms, whatever it is about our lifestyles and popular culture that mandates that we must be entertained with the gore, mayhem, abuse, and the traumas that regulate our daily existence, we will continue to find ourselves victims of children who have learned to normalize the violence of their experiential and virtual realities.

In living made so bleak by racism—when ethnic identity becomes the way one learns to be cautious instead of bold and restrained rather than imaginative—artistry's bold defensive strokes combat the caution and the restraint—either by telling us the stories we have not heard, or in its productive example of an alternative to despair.

Richard Wright's autobiographical novel *Black Boy* researches the lessons of this author's own childhood and traces his evolution into a writer.[36] Richard finds the spiritual and psychical strength to make the kinds of judgments that will save him from falling under the oppressive weight of racism. His salvation comes from an objectifying that has some relationship to the invisibility that figures in Ellison's novel; yet Richard emerges less fractured than the Invisible Man.

> I was now rapidly learning to contain the tension I felt in my relations with whites. . . . It was fairly easy to contemplate the race issue in the shop without reaching those heights of fear that devastated me. A measure of objectivity entered into my observations of white men and women. Either I could stand more mental strain than formerly or I had discovered deep within me ways of handling it. (196)

If children can avoid "the stultifying oppressive messages of depreciation beamed toward [them] by [their] society," they may gain access to a redemptive creativity.[37] bell hooks argues a similar point, noting in *Talking Back* that

> when I ponder the silences, the voices that are not heard, the voices of those wounded and/or oppressed individuals who do not speak or write, I contemplate the acts of persecution, torture—the terrorism that breaks spirits, that makes creativity impossible.[38]

Richard Wright and bell hooks both learned how a writer's voice could cultivate hope as a way of contradicting the despair of childhood. Wright makes a saving connection between ethnicity and ethics. He understood his Southern culture "from which I sprang," as one that could make his blackness a tragedy and a "terror from which I fled" (225). However, the last pages of *Black Boy* make clear both the desperate choices of ethical imperative when colored by ethnic identity as well as their creative potential. "I had felt that nothing short of life itself hung upon each of my actions and decisions . . . [and the] emotional impact of imaginative constructions" (226–227). For Wright, the potentially generative power of a creative spirit was both "promise" and "justification for action" (226–227).

Literary children's lives compellingly illustrate how this is true. Their complicated narratives are not available in the truncated imagery of contemporary media coverage. Our children's stories are despairingly similar. However, the media's images encourage and sustain the racist stereotypes that their magnified faces validate. And these children are absolutely beyond the potential for the creative protection that "emerges from sustained resistance" in part because the coverage they receive controls their identities.[39] Their plights are past healing—creative, spiritual, or otherwise.

Morrison makes it stunningly clear how far past

redemption Cholly has fallen. She does implicate a creative potential that has been lost. His life "could only become coherent in the head of musician" (125). But because he lacked the music of the narrator's intuitive creativity, spiritual and moral coherence were not his due. On the other hand, Claudia and Frieda, the sisters who survive their "degenerative environments" (to use Harris's phrase) in *The Bluest Eye*, learn to listen to their mother's voice for "truth in timbre." The "greens and blues" in her fussing soliloquies save them from despair (18). A similarly creative salvation is posited in Wright's novel where, at critically poignant moments, the despairing narrative breaks and the riff is underscored by lyrical and repetitive narrative junctures that assert his artist's spirit (7–8, 40–41, 63–64).

The contemporary life of Bernice Reagon, a child whose past experiences in civil rights demonstrations were a definitive episode in her life, testifies to the saving grace of creativity:

> Day by day I found courage to be who I was. This was different from people who wanted me to be [remain quiescent]. Taking the risk. There was something about doing things that I had always been warned would kill or ruin you. Well I did get suspended and I did go to jail—things I had been told to avoid at all costs. I saw people die so I knew that some risks could kill . . . but if you stay in the safety zone all the time . . . you'll never know yourself at your most brilliant.[40]

Reagon's is the example of success that literary children, and too many urban children never latch onto—or find within their slim, small reaches. They are like Toni Morrison's Sula, a character Morrison acknowledges needs the form and control of artistry.

> Had she paints, clay, or knew the discipline of the dance, or strings; had she anything to engage her tremendous curiosity and her gift for metaphor, she might have exchanged the restlessness and preoccupation with whim for an activity that provided her with all she yearned for. And like any artist with no form, she became dangerous.[41]

When psychologist Robert Coles first gave Ruby Bridges "paints or clay" (actually it was crayons and paints), and asked her to draw, there was clear evidence of the disabling trauma of her daily experience. A front line citizen in the 1960s move to integrate schools in the south, six-year-old Ruby faced mobs of vicious white folks whose screamed abuses accompanied, along with the state troopers, her long walk into a nearly vacated school building. Coles recorded this about her drawings:

> She did . . . distinguish between white and Negro people. She drew white people larger and more lifelike. Negroes were smaller, their bodies less intact. A white girl we both knew to be her own size appeared several times taller. While Ruby's own face lacked an eye in one drawing, an ear in another, the white girl never lacked any features. Moreover, Ruby drew the white girl's hands and legs carefully, always making sure that they had the proper number of fingers and toes. Not so with her own limbs, or those of any other Negro children she chose (or was asked) to picture. A thumb or forefinger

might be missing, or a whole set of toes. The arms were
shorter, even absent or truncated.[42]

The tragedy of psychic fracture is the sacrifice and loss of self.

Departures

I live constantly with the events and situations of two
worldviews cluttering my own desire for a calm, or at least a
stable, center. But the actual images from one: brief, bleak
clips from the lives of children I will never know, and the
vivid, sustained portraits of literary children whose "luck
and lives"—as Gwendolyn Brooks so poignantly addresses
in "The Mother"—are prosaically sustained in the fiction
that is the stuff of my profession parallel too closely for me
to ignore.

Although it would be courageous to acknowledge that
the moral texture of our children's lives is beyond their control and out of ours, we spend our energies and efforts on
developing a complex web of contradictory behaviors and
expectations that suggest the contrary. We hold on to the
Proverbial message—"Train up a child in the way that he
should go, and he will not depart from it"—but we also too
easily divest ourselves of responsibility in the lives of desperately hurt children. The book of Proverbs has no salve for
those whom a nation has psychologically and spiritually
battered—those whose injuries begin with their color and
sometimes leak into their character.

A call to "Stop the violence" was echoed across this
country following the 1992 rebellion in Los Angeles. This
call is neither an initiatory rally nor a conclusive one. It rests
instead at an unstable center that recognizes violence as both

source and substance in the moral lives of our children, characterizing both their conduct and the codes that define their living. The offenses these youths commit against their families and their communities clearly must be addressed. If they cannot develop a control that keeps us safe, we must be protected from their rage. I do not argue that we use the stories of their lives to absolve them of responsibility—or to avoid and subvert the consequences of their conduct. However, if we do not want to see generation after generation replicate their punishing rage, we had better do more as a morally conscious society than build more prisons or populate our streets with more police. Until we look to the conduct of our cultural lives, the policies of our politics, and the economies of our ethics and then measure all of these against the morals that the streets affirm, the violence will continue, unabated and unaddressed. To bring a halt to this dangerous spiral, we must address the despairing violence of their living with as much energy and effort as we attend to the consequences of their violently destructive lives.

Instead, we continue to nurture without question the very institutions of legal and social agencies whose neglect and ineptitude are so stunningly complicit in our macabre parade of sad, lost, and damaged children. And while we rightfully call for these dangerous children to carry responsibility for their conduct, we fail to hold our institutions and our public policies and cultures responsible. The political agency and monetary authority that we have invested in these social structures leave meager room for the spiritual grace and compassionate attention that would give them the dynamic energy of empowered change. Without the wholeness of compassionate activism, and without a reflective and responsible acknowledgment of the historical cycles of violence within our children's lives, the spectral shadows of racism and its accompanying abuses will continue to linger and lurk around the brilliant flashes of our children's spirits.

In Birmingham and Atlanta, Wappinger Falls, New York (where Tawana Brawley was sacrificed to an abusively constructed public identity), in Los Angeles and in Kalamazoo—wherever color and youth have collaboratively marked the victims—those children who were not directly touched by the violence have been indirectly scarred by their likeness to those who were.

All of us have a collective responsibility in the damaged lives of our children—vulnerable already because of poverty or abuse, blighted schools and schooling, the inequities of health care, or the lack of nourishment and support for their adolescent mothers. They and we are only made more vulnerable by a society that foregrounds violence as entertainment, in which extremes of privacy are easily violated as we democratically support our freedom to cable access, in which casual sexuality is linked to even more casual violence in advertising, and in the preponderance of weapons easily available to anyone.

Yes, I know. Some vulnerable youngsters do not succumb. They, like bell hooks, successfully resist. Other children however, fill the discursive spaces of our national discourse about the fear their behaviors inculcate in our society. Each is unhappily left with the earned consequences of their violence—equitable or not—because their conduct has shoved them aside from the forums where these policies are debated. Each of us must bear responsibility for creating a culture that contributes to our children's dis/ease, and nurtures it rather than healthy, safe, and progressive alternatives. Our children's energies are drained as they fight the fear and terror within our public cultures. Their infancy, childhood, and adolescence are busily spent trying to survive the violent associations we connect to their color and that we force upon their youthful vulnerabilities. We must understand that their potential to nurture a loving and a moral spirit diminishes with each battle waged. They must feel that a creative and redemptive spirituality is within their grasp and that they can mold it to fit their needs. Like Bernice Reagon, whose life outside of the safety zone was protected by her own sure resistance, and Richard Wright, who learned the power of "imaginative construction," our children must be able to form the artistry of their lives. If our children's spiritual lives are not safe and sure, we lose rather than gain the security and safety that allegedly motivate the attention we lavish on their moral lives. Conceiving and believing in the potential of their lives is our children's visionary entitlement. Assuring them this spectacle is our responsibility.

We cannot nurture a community that makes grace and compassion rare rather than abundant qualities. We are all responsible, in this global village, for our children's spirits. The ancestors hold us all in their hands. Without discrimination. We can do no less than their loving example.

A Storied Life

I shall be telling this with a sigh.
    —Robert Frost

With a sigh. I know that heave of air—that loss of volume and capacity. I feel it now, as I close this work, reading it over once again, wondering at my own prescience.

I had decided, several years ago, to write with Robert Coles's title *The Moral Life of Children* in mind. That chapter was intellectually framed over the course of many readings of children's lives in literature. I had no idea then that it would frame itself, indeed clasp itself to my own life, and my child's, so relentlessly.

I reach for the telephone and gaze into the glass in one liquid movement. My child, my son, reaches for the phone as well. We look at each other through the thickened slab of bulletproof glass. His orange jail jumpsuit is louder than our voices. We do not talk much. I touch the glass with my hand, wondering at the melodrama I encourage with this gesture. It seems more like a movie's classic movement than my own. But my son touches back; his large, calloused palm reaches toward mine. Each of us misses this touching.

His life leaked into my studied prose. He is the vulnerable-to-despair child of the last chapter. He is one of the specially selected children who recite "The Creation" before gathered family and churchfolk in the second chapter. He is the absent presence in my reverie about hair.

His head rarely rested against my body in any lingering ritual like the braiding of his sister's hair. But then, I recall now, a dim memory of his first days in our home, after his adoption, when I parted and oiled and massaged his scalp, and turned and twisted his tight spongy hair into mini-dreadlocks. I wanted to urge some life into the dry and neglected head and hair his white foster family had neither known to nor cared to care for. But this brief moment was no ritual. It had no ceremony.

I wonder now if I had touched his head and hair with the same constancy and calm that his sister had as a part of each of her days, would he have felt more certain of my love and more able, with this certainty, to resist the despair. His hair is dry again, I notice now, studying him through the glass. I cannot now reach through the glass—his head is beyond my reach.

This final note appears and disappears on my computer's screen. Armed with cultural tradition and academic practice that enact and enable myriad masking subtleties, I struggle with its inclusion.[1] My deep worry over him only weights the wonder I feel as I watch this child greet the difficult struggle of his life, each day, with such fierce passion. His tenacity is relentlessly assertive—despite daunting, and likely to be overwhelming, circumstances. His deeply loving spirit remains throughout, submerged, protectively, beneath the veil of his own tragically storied life. I constantly feel its urge toward redemption.

This reflection ultimately remains because my anguish, my intellect, my love and my fear each provoked this manuscript. It is here because I want to encourage a humanism that does not abstractly embrace an aesthetic that is so surely and resolutely formed by actual and visceral intersections of grace and pain. These demand of us an intimacy no different from the intimacy between ethical judgment and ethnic identities that our nation and our contemporary lives make both insistent and palpable. These demand as well the "certain height" Frost projects.[2] This is not the height of distance and disdain, but a *certain* height of unfailing perspective where "praise and blame" both mediate and transgress and, in so doing, complicate the narratives that describe our conduct and discern its codes.

Notes

Introduction

1. The phrase is Cornel West's. See his *Race Matters* (Boston: Beacon Press, 1993), esp. chap. 2, "The Pitfalls of Racial Reasoning," 21–32.

2. Stanley Hauerwas, *The Peaceable Kingdom: A Primer in Christian Ethics* (Notre Dame: University of Notre Dame Press, 1983), 21.

3. Edward Said, *The World, the Text, and the Critic* (Cambridge, Mass.: Harvard University Press, 1983), 26.

4. Renita Weems, "African American Women and the Bible," in *Stony the Road We Trod: African American Biblical Interpretation,* ed. Cain Hope Felder (Minneapolis: Fortress Press, 1991), 69, 70.

5. Jervis Anderson, "The Public Intellectual," *The New Yorker* (January 17, 1994): 40.

6. See my discussion of Jean Elshtain in chapter 3, p. 161.

Chapter One. The Body Politic

1. From the Latin "testis," testimony has extended from usage that meant to bear witness to one's virility.

2. Ellis Cose, *The Rage of a Privileged Class* (New York: HarperCollins, 1993), 1.

3. Toni Morrison, "Friday on the Potomac," in *Race-ing Justice, En-Gendering Power* (New York: Pantheon Books, 1992), xiv, xvii.

4. See Henry Louis Gates's discussion of this event in "Writing 'Race and the Difference It Makes,' " in *"Race," Writing, and Difference*, ed. Henry Louis Gates, Jr. (Chicago: University of Chicago Press, 1986), esp. 7—9.

5. The flag-waving, anti-intellectual, and knee-jerk right-wing support that David Brock's *The Real Anita Hill: The Untold Story* (New York: The Free Press, 1993) has received from the conservative right (Rush Limbaugh and Tony Brown are two embarrassingly public examples) attests to the fearful hysteria Hill's bravery aroused. In a personal correspondence, my colleague Cathy Davidson asks a series of relevant and hard-hitting questions about this book: "Why would anyone feel compelled to trash a witness? To write a whole book about her? And why would it become a bestseller?" The subtext of this repulsive book is clearly articulated in Brock's (now publicly retracted) one-liner—that Hill is "a little nutty and a little slutty." The real "told" story is preserved on video. It clearly indicates that in the face of the cameras and in the faces of those white males of the Senate judiciary, Hill's bravery, articulateness, intelligence, honesty, unwavering dignity, and heroism had to be deconstructed.

6. The fact of Hill's color certainly did not escape the text of the hearing. Thomas himself testified that it "played to the worst stereotypes about black men in this country." Commentators evoked legions of history's black women so that the legacy of color was not lost on the reading public. Commentator Nancy Gibbs called Hill "the poised daughter of so many [abused] generations of black women," naming her as the legatee of Harriet Tubman, Sojourner Truth, and Rosa Parks ("An Ugly Circus," *Time* [October 21, 1991]: 35). In the same issue, columnist Jack White recalled sexist reactions to Alice Walker when *The Color Purple* became a national phenomenon and referred to the incredulity given the Tawana Brawley incident. White noted that "black women's complaints about sexist behavior are taken even less seriously than white women's" ("The Stereotyping of Race," 66). Sidney Blumenthal wondered aloud whether then President Bush's "trump card on race" (Clarence Thomas) could be played "when the game is sexual politics" ("The Drifter," *The New Republic* [November 11, 1991]: 24).

7. Lorene Cary, *Black Ice* (New York: Vintage Books, 1991). Citations are noted parenthetically in the text.

8. bell hooks, *Black Looks: Race and Representation* (Boston: South End Press, 1992).

9. Ibid., 79–80, 82.

10. Toni Morrison, *Song of Solomon* (New York: Signet, 1977). Citations from this edition are noted parenthetically in the text.

11. Gloria Naylor, *Linden Hills* (New York: Penguin, 1985). Citations from this edition are noted parenthetically in the text.

12. Patricia Williams, *The Alchemy of Race and Rights* (Cambridge, Mass.: Harvard University Press, 1991), 229.

13. Jacques Lacan, "The Mirror Stage," in *A Critical and Cultural Theory Reader*, ed. Antony Easthope and Kate McGowen (Toronto: University of Toronto Press, 1992), 74. For an extended discussion of the mirror's imagery and its intimate connection to voice and body, see Karla Holloway, "Holy Heat, Rituals of the Spirit in Hurston's *Their Eyes Were Watching God*," *Journal of Religion and Literature* 23 (Autumn 1991): 127–141.

14. Williams, *Alchemy*, 235, 236.

15. Alice Walker, *The Color Purple* (New York: Harcourt Brace Jovanovich, 1982), 3. Citations from this edition are noted parenthetically in the text.

16. I am indebted here to Patricia Williams's discussion in *Alchemy* for the focus of this reflection.

17. Toni Morrison, *The Bluest Eye* (New York: Holt, Rinehart and Winston, 1970). Citations from this edition are noted parenthetically in the text.

18. The mirror displaces the phallus here, although the descriptive context encourages its trace on the narrative—she "stick[s]" it between her legs. It is a moment that argues for those who take issue with Lacan's privileging the phallus as a governing signifier, and this is an issue that makes very clear the way in which the failure to consider race and class undermine theory and illustrate what Anthony Appiah would likely label as theory's often meager evidential terrain. In this instance, the phallic privilege

loses its structure (I consciously signify on the signifier) because rather than the mirror's thrust bringing any gendered identity to this moment, Celie's voice—her language—and its engagement with the language of her body inscribe the occasion. Syntactically, each of these structures (I take, I stand, I lie, I haul, I stick) avoids the copula—instantiating an indirect, but nevertheless poignant displacement of the phallus as signifier. Consequently, this event does not engage *jouissance* beyond the phallus (Lacan); it is instead *jouissance* despite the phallus.

19. See Karla Holloway, *Moorings and Metaphors: Figures of Culture and Gender in Black Women's Literature* (New Brunswick, N.J.: Rutgers University Press, 1992), esp. chap. 2, "The Novel Politics of Literary Interpretation."

20. Angela Y. Davis, *Women, Culture, and Politics* (New York: Random House, 1984), 45.

21. See "Lani Guinier by Vint Lawrence," *The New Republic* (June 14, 1993): 18; and Donald Baer, "The Trials of Lani Guinier," *U.S. News and World Report* (June 7, 1993): 38. Baer predicts that with Guinier's "strange name, strange hair, [and] strange ideas—she's history" (38).

22. Holloway, *The Character of the Word: The Texts of Zora Neale Hurston* (Westport, Conn.: Greenwood Press, 1987), xiv.

23. Zora Neale Hurston, *Seraph on the Suwanee* (New York: Charles Scribner's Sons, 1948).

24. Zora Neale Hurston, *Dust Tracks on a Road* (1942; reprint, New York: Harper Perennial, 1991).

25. hooks, *Black Looks*, 80–81.

26. "Noted Novelist Denies She 'Abused' 10-Year-Old-Boy," *New York Age* (October 23, 1948).

27. "Boys 10 Accuse Zora," *Baltimore Afro-American* (October 23, 1948).

28. The incident I speak of occurred at a Fall 1985 conference in Urbana, Illinois, honoring Hurston. The panelist whose comment provoked such passioned response was African American literary critic Blyden Jackson.

29. Luce Irigaray, *This Sex Which Is Not One*, trans. Cather-

ine Porter with Caroline Burke (Ithaca: Cornell University Press, 1985), 31, 33.

30. bell hooks, "Writing the Subject: Reading the Color Purple," in *Reading Black, Reading Feminist*, ed. Henry Louis Gates, Jr. (New York: Meridian, 1990), 455, 456.

31. Ibid., 467.

32. I am thinking specifically of Nella Larsen's *Passing*. The best insight into this closeted subtext of the novel may be found in Deborah McDowell's introduction to the Rutgers University Press edition of *Quicksand and Passing* (1928, 1929; reprint, New Brunswick, N.J.: Rutgers University Press, 1988). See also McDowell's earlier consideration of the issue of lesbianism in black women's literatures: "New Directions for Black Feminist Criticism," *The New Feminist Criticism*, ed. Elaine Showalter (New York: Pantheon, 1985), 186–199. This essay, a response to Barbara Smith's "Toward a Black Feminist Criticism" (also in Showalter, 168–185), represents a sea change for the insights that come in the Rutgers University Press edition of Larsen's work. The critical silence that has met (for example) Anne Schockley's fiction (see esp. *Loving Her* [Indianapolis: Bobbs-Merrill, 1974]) indicates the closeting that accompanies the publication of lesbian literatures by black women. The conflicted reception of Audre Lorde within the academy of black studies is example both of the exception and the rule.

33. Julie Dash with Toni Cade Bambara and bell hooks, *Daughters of the Dust: The Making of an African American Woman's Film* (New York: The New Press, 1992), 83.

34. Ibid., 67.

35. Gloria Naylor, *The Women of Brewster Place* (New York: Penguin Books, 1983). Citations from this edition are noted parenthetically in the text.

36. Zora Neale Hurston, *Their Eyes Were Watching God* (1937; reprint, Urbana: University of Illinois Press, 1978). Citations in the text are from this edition.

37. Morrison, "Friday," xxii, xxiii.

38. Davis, *Women, Culture, and Politics*, 45.

39. Ibid.

40. Ibid., 35–37.

41. Hurston, *Dust Tracks*, 192.

42. My discussion of this event is based upon my reading of Sander Gilman, "Black Bodies, White Bodies: Toward an Iconography of Female Sexuality in Late Nineteenth-Century Art, Medicine, and Literature" in *"Race," Writing, and Difference*, ed. Gates, 223–261. Direct citations within the following paragraphs are from Gilman (232).

43. I leave a blank space for her name, rather than using the given name of her European kidnappers. My intent is to signify, in this manner, the loss of her familial given name as she experienced the victimization of anthropological inquiry.

Chapter Two. Language, Thought, and Culture

1. Marilyn Milloy, "Angelou, Poetry Both Hits Peers Say," *The Raleigh News and Observer* (January 21, 1993): 5A. These comments were made by poet Louis Rubin.

2. David Nicholson, "Poetic Justice and Other Clichés," *American Visions* 8 (August/September 1993): 26–27.

3. James Weldon Johnson, "The Creation," in *God's Trombones: Seven Negro Sermons in Verse* (New York: The Viking Press, 1927).

4. Sororities and social clubs within middle and upper class African American communities continue the trend developed in the early to mid-century to have cotillions and debutante balls for their children. The inability of African American youngsters to participate in like events held in white communities was at least a partial reason for its emergence in black communities. John Oliver Killens's novel *Cotillion: Or One Good Bull is Worth Half the Herd* (1971) parodies this event.

5. I find it interesting to hear discussion of black oratory as if it were a genetic trait among black folk that speaking skills are held in such high esteem. It is important to note on the record that this is a practiced and developed artistry. Skill, talent, and work are its components. Culturally, the work that goes into oratorical artistry is highly respected within the black community.

6. Known as the "Ann Arbor Decision," this case involved the school district of Ann Arbor, Michigan, and the parents of children in a local elementary school. Testimony of several noted linguists (Geneva Smitherman among them), parents, and teachers eventually led to the judicial decision that teachers' misinformation and poor education about dialect differences did contribute to the academic failure of children who spoke nonstandard, black-identified dialects in the school. The court's decision that children were indeed handicapped by their teachers' linguistic biases led to its instruction that the district arrange in-service workshops on sociolinguistic awareness and educational practice that would address and correct their educational deficiencies in this area.

7. Mari Matsuda, "Voices of America: Accent, Anti-discrimination Law, and a Jurisprudence of the Last Reconstruction," *Yale Law Journal* 100 (1991): 1329–1407. See esp. p. 1402.

8. See Michael Dyson, *Reflecting Black: African-American Cultural Criticism* (Minneapolis: University of Minnesota Press, 1993) for an especially cogent discussion of Lee's film.

9. Toni Morrison, "On the Backs of Blacks," *Time* Special Issue, "The New Face of America" (Fall 1993): 57.

10. I have talked with more people who disagree with me on this issue of attaching Smiley's potential agency to his gender and his color than I have met with those who agree with me. I include the point here because I do still believe the issues of color and gender play a significant role within and without the black community, and I want to encourage the argument and discussion this point has already encouraged among my friends and colleagues.

11. The issues of race and culture as they affect public policy decisions about language use and its legislation have been addressed in a pamphlet developed by the Language Policy Committee of the Conference on College Composition. The focus in this publication is to highlight the recent attention devoted to English Only/English Plus movements and to make clear the restrictive, racist, and unconstitutional stance of English Only legislation. Copies of the pamphlet can be obtained from the CCCC, 1111 Kenyon Road, Urbana, IL.

12. Morrison, "On the Backs of Blacks."

13. For a discussion of dialect differences and children's literacy, see essays within the section "Language" in *Tapping Potential: English Language Arts for the Black Learner*, ed. Charlotte K. Brooks (Urbana: National Council of Teachers of English, 1985), 7–83.

14. Only when linguistics gets affixed to "socio-" do attitudes about language and dialect differences come into play. As a purely scientific explanation of language difference, expressive and performed language (speech) is not considered to be an evaluative measure of proficiency or knowledge of its cognitive base (competence).

15. The most hotly contested debate in the academy on speech, class, race, and ability happened when a British researcher, Basil Bernstein, indicated that a difference between working class and middle class mothers' language in Great Britain could be explained with his illustration that the former spoke to their children in "restricted codes" and the latter used an "elaborate code" in conversation. These terms were first generalized to suggest sentence length and syntactic complexity, then stretched to include thinking ability and depth. Finally, they were generalized to a whole population of language users in the United States—black and white speakers of English. A thorough review of the research and the arguments that contested its original findings and its generalization to blacks and whites in this country may be found in Nancy Ainsworth Johnson's *Current Topics in Language* (Cambridge, Mass.: Winthrop Publishers, Inc., 1976). See esp. Johnson's essay, "The Research Non-Basis for 'Restricted Codes,' " 203–220.

16. The exchange I refer to was on C-SPAN, a call-in segment televised on December 9, 1993.

17. Sharon Epperson and Jay Peterzell, "Enforcing Correctness," *Time* 143 (February 7, 1994): 37.

18. Ibid.

19. Naylor, *Linden Hills*.

20. This characteristic of hypercorrect speech is a sociolinguistic phenomenon in ethnic communities whose speech differences are considered "basilects"—dialects at the lower end of the prestige scale. In an effort to rid their language of this social barrier

to respect and status, speaking patterns assume hypercorrect features (exaggerated pronunciation of word endings, absence of contractions, etc.). An acrolect in the English-speaking world, that is, a dialect at the upper end of the social scale, would be RP (received pronunciation) British English—spoken by the upper classes of Great Britain.

21. Alice Walker, *The Third Life of Grange Copeland* (New York: Pocket Books, 1988). Citations from this edition are noted parenthetically in the text.

22. Maya Angelou, *I Know Why the Caged Bird Sings* (New York: Bantam, 1971). Citations from this edition are noted parenthetically in the text.

23. Wernor Sollors, *The Invention of Ethnicity* (New York: Oxford University Press, 1989), xi. See esp. xi–xvii.

24. I am indebted to Maurice O. Wallace of Duke University's English department for this phrasing and the thoughtful reflection it characterizes.

25. Martha Bayles, "Malcolm X and the Hip Hop Culture," *Reconstruction* 2 (1993): 100–103. Bayles writes that there are "positive rap groups that abjure the sheer moral ugliness of gangster rap—they do not, for example, boast about their mighty 'dicks' ripping asunder the bodies of 'bitches' and 'ho's' " (102).

26. A flurry of op-ed pieces followed Gates's testimony for the defense. Most disputed, with varying degrees of argumentative intensity, Gates's claims about the "great virtuosity" of 2 Live Crew. Among the more sustained responses was law professor Kimberle Crenshaw's "Beyond Racism and Misogyny: Black Feminism and 2 Live Crew" published in the December 1991 edition of the *Boston Review*. Crenshaw took issue with the defense's bad faith failure to distinguish between the ethnic artistry of *As Nasty as They Wanna Be* (which, unlike me, she concedes—albeit begrudgingly) and the representational damage/danger to black women in 2 Live Crew's violent phallocentrism. Crenshaw finds the album's misogyny and Gates's defense of it "criminal" in a manner that has less to do with jurisprudence than with culture. For further treatments of gangster rap and the problem of ethnic authenticity, see also Anne Clark, " 'As Nasty as They Wanna Be': Popular Music on Trial,"

New York University Law Review 65 (December 1990): 1481–1531; Michael Eric Dyson, "2 Live Crews's Rap: Sex, Race and Class," *Christian Century* 108 (January 2, 1991): 7–8; Lisa Jones, "The Signifying Monkees," *Village Voice* 35 (November 6, 1990): 43–47; and Alan Light, "About Salary or Reality?—Rap's Recurrent Conflict," *South Atlantic Quarterly* 90 (Fall 1991): 855–870.

27. Luther Campbell and John R. Miller, *As Nasty as They Wanna Be: The Uncensored Story of Luther Campbell of the 2 Live Crew* (Fort Lee, N.J.: Barricade Books, 1992).

28. Ibid., 156.

29. Ibid., 158.

30. Houston Baker, *Black Studies, Rap, and the Academy* (Chicago: University of Chicago Press, 1993), 5.

31. Ibid.

32. Ibid., 5, 22.

33. Dyson, *Reflecting Black*, 4.

34. See Gayl Jones's discussion of the effect and focus of dialect poetry in *Liberating Voices* (New York: Penguin Books, 1991), 57.

35. See William H. Robinson, *Early Black American Poetry* (Dubuque, Iowa: William Brown Co., 1969). The complete text of "Ol' Doc' Hyar" can be found on pages 263–264 of this collection.

36. Ibid., 262.

37. Stephen Henderson, *Understanding the New Black Poetry* (New York: William Morrow & Company, Inc., 1972).

38. Ibid., 46, 47.

39. One striking example of the controversy that arises between a community's aesthetic codes and an artist's imaginative freedom occurred with the outcry against Alice Walker's novel *The Color Purple* and the filmed version directed by Steven Spielberg. See chap. 1, "My Tongue is in My Friend's Mouth," for a discussion of this novel and the controversy it occasioned.

40. Bayles, "Malcolm X and the Hip Hop Culture," 101.

41. "Smitherman Says Current Students Challenge the Mainstream," *The Council Chronicle* (NCTE Newsletter) 3 (November 1993): 6.

42. Ibid.

43. Bayles, "Malcolm X and the Hip Hop Culture," 103.

44. Nicholson, "Poetic Justice and Other Clichés," 26.

45. Charlotte Hawkins Brown, *The Correct Thing To Do To Say To Wear* (Boston: Christopher Publishing House, 1941). The preface to *The Correct Thing* explains its purpose:

> an etiquette guide used in cultural education at Palmer and elsewhere. Through it and other means Dr. Brown (founder and president of Palmer Memorial Institute—a residential prepatory school for black youth in Sedalia, N.C. that was founded in 1902) promoted her vision of education which would enable black children to become, as she put it, "educationally efficient, religiously sincere, and culturally secure."

Palmer educated many members of my own family, including my grandfather, Claudie D'Arcy Clapp, whose diplomas from the "Grammar School Course" and "Higher Course," both signed by Charlotte Hawkins (Brown), hang in my home. His education at Palmer in 1911 and 1914 prepared him for the degree he earned at Meharry Pharmaceutical School (Nashville, Tenn.) in 1916.

46. Bridgette A. Lacy, "Life's Lesson Remembered," *The Raleigh News and Observer* (November 16, 1993): 1E.

47. Baker, *Black Studies*, 96.

Chapter Three. The Moral Lives of Children

1. Ken Magid and Carole A. McKelvey, *High Risk Children Without a Conscience* (New York: Bantam, 1987), 22, 26. Of note to this discussion is the professional background of the collaborative team that authored this book. At the time of its publication, Magid was chief of psychological services at Golden Medical Clinic in Colorado and Carole McKelvey was a journalist. Their joint effort underscores one of my concerns—that the popular press appeal of these stories encourages the kind of casual dissociation that phrases like "without a conscience" produce.

2. Joby Warrick, "Children on the Edge: Violent Cases Shock a City," *The Raleigh News and Observer* (May 18, 1993): 7A. Reporters for this series obtained a waiver that bypassed laws

designed to protect juvenile privacy. They were allowed to sit in on hearings and testimony that are usually closed to the public. Photographs of the children (not their faces) were generously used. Although the names of children were changed, ostensibly to protect their privacy, enough of their life stories was included to subvert this intent. Whether the public's "need to know" was more important than the children's "right-to-privacy" was a decision the children could not make. Their situations, as well as their class, culture, and community, assured that they would be unimportant in whatever decision-making process was used to divest them of their rights.

3. As I make these assessments about adoption, I acknowledge that there are white families who face barriers in adopting black children. The National Association of Black Social Workers has been consistent in a two-decade-long argument against this process and I agree with their reservations. As long as culture and community matter in America, we cannot decide that children who are already at risk, and whose family structures may cause them another level of psychological adjustment, are best served by being adopted by whites. I do, albeit reluctantly, concede that children in foster care would be better off adopted by any loving family. I make this concession with reluctance because of my own familiarity with the abuses that can go unchecked and unfettered in the foster care system. Infants and children new to the (foster care) system would be safer—both psychologically and socially—if they were raised in black families. My family's experience with bi-racial placements within the foster care system (black children into white families) makes me absolutely inflexible with any other arrangement.

4. Editorial, "How to End the Killing of Our Children," *The Chicago Tribune* (December 26, 1993): 2C.

5. Both youngsters who will be tried for the murder of James Jordan are ethnic minorities. One is African American; the other has Native American ancestry.

6. A story that journalist Leslie Stahl has told in some public gatherings illustrates the misappropriated appeal of the visual in the media. Stahl relates a story about a piece she prepared during the Reagan/Carter presidential election designed to show the mismatch between Reagan's version of a democratic and free

America and the impact of his administration's policies on America's underclass. Her voiced text pointed out these inequities. The visual text showed pristine, comfy, and bucolic images from Reagan's own "Morning in America" political commercials—flag-waving, family reunions, parades, and picnics. Stahl was later thanked by the Republican party operatives (specifically the Reagan campaign director) for her pro-Reagan newspiece. No one even listened to her text, she was told—they were caught up in the powerful and appealing visual images. Later review of the piece before focus groups revealed exactly that bias—that the visual easily replaced the voiced text.

7. One exception to the run of tourist-killed-by-blacks stories was the attention devoted to Christopher Wilson. Wilson, a thirty-two-year-old New York City brokerage clerk, was visiting his mother in West Palm Beach, Florida, on New Year's Day, 1993. Two day laborers from nearby Lakeland, Florida, accosted Wilson, taunted him with racial slurs, doused him with gasoline, and set him afire. The perpetrators, Mark Kohut and Charles Rourke, were arrested, tried, and later found guilty of attempted murder. Appropriately labeled a "hate crime" against another tourist (but this time, the race of victim and perpetrator were reversed), this story did receive significant play in the media. Some thought the attention directed toward this event was an attempt to ameliorate the effect of the multiple stories about black youths who attacked white and foreign tourists during the same period. The racial-reversal and the tourist dimension were significant to news coverage of the event and the commentary on Court TV, which co   ed the trial of Kohut and Rourke.

8. Cornel West, *Race Matters*, xi.

9. Brent Staples, "Into the White Ivory Tower," *New York Times Magazine* (February 6, 1994): 22.

10. Ibid., 44.

11. Toni Morrison, *The Bluest Eye* (New York: Holt, Rinehart and Winston, 1970). Citations from this edition are noted parenthetically in the text.

12. Trudier Harris, *Fiction and Folklore: The Novels of Toni Morrison* (Knoxville: University of Tennessee Press, 1992), 19.

13. Claudia L. Jewett, *Helping Children Cope with Separation and Loss* (Cambridge, Mass.: The Harvard Common Press, 1982). See esp. 106–108 and 117–119.

14. I identify mothers, not fathers, as the "guests" on this program and others like it because they are the ones who are convinced and asked to share their stories. The talk show audience is largely female—both within and outside of the studio, so this match of genders is explainable in that configuration. However, I think it worth noting that those who receive the interrogation are often mothers. Fathers largely escape, for whatever reasons, the public confrontation and critical interrogation.

15. Jean Elshtain, *Power Trips and Other Journeys: Essays in Feminism as Civic Discourse* (Madison: University of Wisconsin Press, 1990), 54.

16. See the collected essays on adolescent pregnancy and childbearing in Anne Lawson and Deborah Rhode, eds., *The Politics of Pregnancy: Adolescent Sexuality and Public Policy* (New Haven: Yale University Press, 1993). Although several essays in this collection argue against the moralistic and paternalistic perspectives that (perhaps too easily) condemn adolescent childbearing, Margaret C. Sims, in "Adolescent Pregnancy Among Blacks," views the debate (about paternalism and morality) "with amazement." Sims refuses to divest the policy issue of its racialized outcomes writing that "today the majority of black children live in single-parent families, most with their mothers. Three-fifths of black children are born out of wedlock. For these children, the future can be fairly bleak. They are likely to live their entire lives in single-parent families, and approximately two-thirds of them will live in poverty. In addition, some recent research suggests that these conditions, in combination, will mean that black children are increasingly likely to be at risk of low educational attainment, involvement in crime, early parenthood, unstable marital relations in later life, and other unfavorable outcomes" (244).

17. Ibid., 244, 243.

18. bell hooks, *Talking Back: Thinking Feminist, Thinking Black* (Boston, Mass.: South End Press, 1989), 7.

19. Ibid.

20. James Baldwin, *Go Tell It on the Mountain* (New York: Alfred A. Knopf, 1953). Citations from this edition are noted parenthetically in the text.

21. During that period black male suicide rates increased from 8 per 100,000 in 1970 to 12 per 100,000 in 1990. Black female rates decreased from 2.6 per 100,000 to 2.3 in the same period. White male suicides increased from 18 to 22 per 100,000 during the same period; white female rates declined slightly. In an ironically placed "Lifestyle" report on suicide (*Newsweek* [April 18, 1994]: 45–49), David Gelman includes demographers' speculations that "the increase among blacks . . . might be because suicide is part of the continuum of violence and despair that surrounds many of them" (48). Orlando Patterson's discussion of the gender crisis in African American relationships includes these notations on suicide so that he might draw a critical attention to the greater rate of suicides among African American males aged fifteen to twenty-four (almost five times greater than women). Patterson's thesis interrogates the assumption of the greater "double-burden" of racism and sexism that black women in America experience. See Orlando Patterson, "Blacklash: The Crisis of Gender Relations Among African Americans," *Transition* 62(1994):4–26, esp. 9–10.

22. Robert Coles, *Children of Crisis Volume I: A Study of Courage and Fear* (Boston: Little, Brown, and Company, 1964), 322.

23. Dudley Randall, "Ballad of Birmingham," in *The Black Poets*, ed. D. Randall (New York: Bantam, 1971), 143–144.

24. Morrison, *Song of Solomon.*

25. Alice Walker, *Possessing the Secret of Joy* (New York: Harcourt, Brace, Jovanovich, 1992). Citations from this edition are noted parenthetically in the text.

26. Richard Perry, *Montgomery's Children* (San Diego, Calif.: Harcourt, Brace, Jovanovich, 1984). Citations from this edition are noted parenthetically in the text.

27. William H. Grier and Price Cobbs, *Black Rage* (New York: Basic Books, 1968), 138.

28. Magid and McKelvey, *High Risk Children*, 26.

29. Grier and Cobbs, *Black Rage*, 164–165.

30. Ibid., 153.

31. Ibid., 180.

32. Harris, *Fiction and Folklore*, 40.

33. Ralph Ellison, *Invisible Man* (1947; reprint, New York: Vintage Books, 1972). Citations from this edition are noted parenthetically in the text.

34. Patricia Williams, *Alchemy of Race*, 169.

35. Ibid., 171.

36. Richard Wright, *Black Boy* (New York: Harper and Brothers Publishers, 1937). Citations from this edition are noted parenthetically in the text.

37. Grier and Cobbs, *Black Rage*, 165.

38. hooks, *Talking Back*, 7–8.

39. Ibid., 8.

40. Audreen Buffalo, "Sweet Honey: A Capella Activists," *Ms.* 3 (March/April 1993): 24–29.

41. Toni Morrison, *Sula* (New York: Alfred A. Knopf, 1974), 121.

42. Coles, *Children of Crisis*, 47.

Epilogue

1. I am recalling here the first lines of Paul Laurence Dunbar's poem "We Wear the Mask."

> We wear the mask that grins and lies,
> It hides our cheeks and shades our eyes,
> This debt we pay to human guile;
> With torn and bleeding hearts we smile,
> And mouth with myriad subtleties.

2. Robert Frost, "Choose Something Like a Star" in *Literature: An Introduction to Reading and Writing*, eds., Edgar V. Roberts and Henry E. Jacobs (New Jersey: Prentice-Hall, 1986), 910–911. These lines especially provoke this reflection:

> It asks of us a certain height . . .
> So when at times the mob is swayed

To carry praise or blame too far,
We may choose something like a star
To stay our minds on, and be staid.

I also think here of the celestial metaphors this reverie joins that seem to frame my life and work. I recalled them in my 1987 Preface to *The Character of the Word*, where I wrote that writing that book was so I could "claim for my children a tradition of astronomical metaphors" (xiii). My grandmother's admonition ("Hitch your wagon to a star") was like what Lucy Hurston told her daughter Zora Neale ("Jump at the sun").

Index

community, African American,
140; history of, 6; identity in,
7, 10; presence and practice
of, 6
competence: and color, 25; and
language, 92, 93, 94, 101,
204*n14*; and performance, 92;
and sexism, 26
conduct: codes of, 96, 175; ethical, 6, 7; moral, 176; "proper,"
15, 16, 17, 133, 134, 207*n45*;
public, 60, 133, 134; ra-
cialized codes of, 109
conflict: of credibility, 26; cultural, 5, 91; linguistic, 45;
psychic, 41
consciousness: critical, 9; private, 45
"Cop Killer" (Ice T), 121
Cosby Show, The (TV series), 123,
124
Cose, Ellis, 20
"Creation, The" (Johnson),
78–80
credibility: conflict of, 26; mea-
suring, 27; and sexism, 27
Crenshaw, Kimberle, 205*n26*
crime, 142; against blacks, 152–
153, 209*n7*; demographics,
147; stereotypes in, 151, 152
cultural: affirmation, 5; artistry,
105; capitalism, 119; codes,
80, 85; conflict, 5, 91; criticism, 8; difference, 86, 88,
111; disadvantage, 91; discourse, 120; diversity, 84; economics, 131; enforcement of
stereotypes, 38; expressivity,

122; history of rap, 109; identity, 8–9, 83, 84, 111, 117;
language, 123; pluralism, 7;
politics, 27, 38, 83; relativism, 172; tradition, 107,
134; values, 121
culture: of abuse, 130; Afrocentric, 118; commodification
of, 105, 108, 119, 120, 121,
122, 126; contemporary, 122;
ethics in, 6; and language,
83, 84, 91; popular, 87, 119;
private, 120; public, 55, 69,
120, 142; race talk in, 87

Dangerous: The Short Films, 128,
129
Danson, Ted, 67, 68, 69
Dash, Julie, 58
Daughters of the Dust (film), 58
Davis, Angela, 45, 46, 60–61,
147
Davis, Ossie, 138
"Deep River" (spiritual), 135
Denny, Reginald, 179
Designing Women (TV series), 125
difference, 58; bodily, 70; cultural, 8–9, 86, 88, 111, 121;
economic, 86; human, 14; language, 204*n14*; linguistic,
88; misuse of, 14; political,
86; racial, 7
discourse: cultural, 120; oppositional, 11; political, 96; racial, 5, 6
District of Columbia, 8
Donahue, Phil, 57
Do the Right Thing (film), 87–91

About the Author

Karla F. C. Holloway is a professor of English and African American literature at Duke University. Her essays on linguistics, literary theory, and cultural studies have appeared in a variety of journals and edited collections. She is the author of *Moorings and Metaphors: Figures of Culture and Gender in Black Women's Literature,* which received a 1993 CHOICE Outstanding Academic Book Award and the 1994 Creative Scholarship Award from the College Language Association; *The Character of the Word: The Texts of Zora Neale Hurston;* and coauthor of *New Dimensions of Spirituality: A BiRacial and BiCultural Reading of the Novels of Toni Morrison.* She is currently working on a documentary study titled *Passed On: African American Mourning Stories.*